An Annotated Critical Bibliography of Thomas Hardy

Harvester Annotated Critical Bibliographies

This major new series provides extensive guides to literary movements and to major figures in English literature. Each volume is edited by a scholar of international repute, and writings by authors and the location of manuscript collections are presented in detail together with information on the secondary writings of each author.

Available

An Annotated Critical Bibliography of Modernism
Alistair Davies

An Annotated Critical Bibliography of Henry James
Nicola Bradbury

An Annotated Critical Bibliography of Milton
C. A. Patrides

An Annotated Critical Bibliography of Feminist Criticism
Maggie Humm

An Annotated Critical Bibliography of George Eliot
George Levine

An Annotated Critical Bibliography of James Joyce
Thomas Staley

An Annotated Critical Bibliography of Jacobean and Caroline Comedy (excluding Shakespeare)
Peter Corbin and Douglas Sedge

An Annotated Critical Bibliography of Thomas Hardy
R. P. Draper and Martin Ray

Forthcoming

An Annotated Critical Bibliography of Tennyson
Marion Shaw

An Annotated Critical Bibliography of Browning
Philip Drew

An Annotated Critical Bibliography of Augustan Poetry
David Noakes and Janet Barron

An Annotated Critical Bibliography of Langland
Derek Pearsall

An Annotated Critical Bibliography of William Morris
David and Sheila Latham

An Annotated Critical Bibliography of Thomas Hardy

Ronald P. Draper
Martin S. Ray

Department of English,
University of Aberdeen

HARVESTER WHEATSHEAF

New York London Toronto Sydney Tokyo

First published 1989 by
Harvester Wheatsheaf
66 Wood Lane End, Hemel Hempstead
Hertfordshire, HP2 4RG
A division of
Simon & Schuster International Group

Printed and bound in Great Britain by
Billing and Sons Ltd, Worcester.

British Library Cataloguing in Publication Data

Draper, R. P. (Ronald Philip), *1928–*
An annotated critical bibliography of
Thomas Hardy – (Harvester annotated critical
bibliographies series)
1. Fiction in English. Hardy Thomas, 1840–
1928. Bibliographies
I. Title   II. Ray, Martin, *1955–*
016,823'8

ISBN 0-7108-1010-5

---

1 2 3 4 5   93 92 91 90 89

Contents

Advice to the Reader

This bibliography gives a selective survey of Hardy scholarship and criticism. Full bibliographic details of each selected item are followed by an evaluative and descriptive summary of its contents. From the increasingly large quantity of criticism about Hardy and his works, only the more substantial and important contributions have been chosen for inclusion.

The seventeen sections cover all major aspects of Hardy criticism. Items within each section or subsection are arranged alphabetically, but numbered in continuous sequence throughout the volume from 1–724. References in the three indexes (based on authorship, subject matter and titles respectively) are to those numbered items, and within particular items numbers in brackets provide cross-references to other related items. By this means it is hoped that the reader will be able to locate easily and quickly comments on any aspect of Hardy's work which may be of special interest. The subject index especially provides a detailed guide to the major themes and areas of Hardy criticism.

Acknowledgement

We would like to express our gratitude to
Miss Andrea Budd and Mrs Aileen Pittendrigh
for typing the manuscript for this book.

Abbreviations

DR	Desperate Remedies
UGT	Under the Greenwood Tree
PBE	A Pair of Blue Eyes
FMC	Far From the Madding Crowd
HE	The Hand of Ethelberta
RN	The Return of the Native
TM	The Trumpet-Major
L	A Laodicean
TT	Two on a Tower
MC	The Mayor of Casterbridge
W	The Woodlanders
T	Tess of the d'Urbervilles
JO	Jude the Obscure
WB	The Well-Beloved
D	The Dynasts
H	Thomas Hardy

Recent Editions

1   (i) NEW WESSEX EDITION (London: Macmillan 1974–78; New York: St Martin's Press, 1975–79)

A very high standard of Introductions. Very useful annotation. Not, however, a proper textual edition.

Far From the Madding Crowd, intro. by John Bayley (London: 1975; New York: 1978).

Jude the Obscure, intro. by Terry Eagleton (London: 1974; New York: 1977).

The Life and Death of the Mayor of Casterbridge, intro. by Ian Gregor (London: 1974; New York: 1977).

The Trumpet-Major, intro. by Barbara Hardy (London: 1974; New York: 1977).

The Return of the Native, intro. by Derwent May (London: 1974; New York: 1978).

Tess of the d'Urbervilles, intro. by P. N. Furbank (London: 1974; New York: 1978).

The Woodlanders, intro. by David Lodge (London: 1974; New York: 1978).

Desperate Remedies, intro. by C. J. P. Beatty (London: 1975; New York: 1977).

The Hand of Ethelberta, intro. by Robert Gittings (London: 1975; New York: 1978).

A Laodicean, intro. by Barbara Hardy (London: 1975; New York: 1978).

A Pair of Blue Eyes, intro. by Ronald Blythe (London: 1975; New York: 1979).

Two on a Tower, intro. by F. B. Pinion (London: 1975; New York: 1977).

Under the Greenwood Tree, intro. by Geoffrey Grigson (London: 1975; New York: 1977).

The Well-Beloved, intro. by J. Hillis Miller (London: 1975; New York: 1978;.

The Stories of Thomas Hardy, ed. F. B. Pinion. I. *Wessex Tales and A Group of Noble Dames* (London: 1977; New York: 1978); II. *Life's Little Ironies and A Changed Man and Other Tales* (London: 1977; New York: 1978); III. *Old Mrs. Chundle and Other Stories with The Famous Tragedy of the Queen of Cornwall* (London: 1977; New York: 1978).

The Complete Poems of Thomas Hardy, ed. James Gibson (London: 1976; New York: 1978).
The Dynasts, ed. Harold Orel (London: 1978; New York: 1978).

(ii) PENGUIN ENGLISH LIBRARY (Harmondsworth: Penguin Books, 1979–81)

A close rival to the *New Wessex Edition* in its excellent introductions, annotations and reasonable price.
The Distracted Preacher and Other Tales, ed. Susan Hill (1979).
Far from the Madding Crowd, ed. Ronald Blythe (1979).
Jude the Obscure, ed. C. H. Sisson (1979).
The Mayor of Casterbridge, ed. Martin Seymour-Smith (1979).
The Return of the Native, ed. George Woodcock (1979).
Tess of the d'Urbervilles, intro. by Al Alvarez, ed. David Skilton (1979).
Under the Greenwood Tree, ed. David Wright (1979).
The Woodlanders, intro. by Ian Gregor, ed. James Gibson (1981).

(iii) WORLD'S CLASSICS (Oxford: Oxford University Press, 1985–   )

Excellent introductions and annotation. Exceptional in the attention paid to the status of the text, each novel being thoroughly revised.
A Pair of Blue Eyes, ed. Alan Manford.
Jude the Obscure, ed. Patricia Ingham.
Under the Greenwood Tree, ed. Simon Gatrell.
The Woodlanders, ed. Dale Kramer.

2   Coleman, Terry (ed.)
AN INDISCRETION IN THE LIFE OF AN HEIRESS
(London: Hutchinson, 1976)

Another edition of H's uncollected work.

3   Grindle, Juliet and Gatrell, Simon (eds)
TESS OF THE D'URBERVILLES (Oxford: Clarendon Press, 1983)

Outstanding textual edition. Uses manuscript of novel as copy text and restores H's original punctuation. Records substantive variants in subsequent editions. This edition is a feat of truly admirable scholarship.

4   Kramer, Dale (ed.)
     THE WOODLANDERS (Oxford: Clarendon Press, 1981)

A textual edition, the first complete study of the evolution of a novel by H. Kramer has collated nine versions of *W* to establish his reliable text. Prints variants in appendices. Though not designed for the lay reader, this is a landmark in the new study of H's texts.

5   Purdy, R. L. (ed.)
     OUR EXPLOITS AT WEST POLEY (London: Oxford University Press, 1952) (1978)

H's story for boys was written in 1883. Previously uncollected.

6   Weber, Carl J. (ed.)
     AN INDISCRETION IN THE LIFE OF AN HEIRESS (Baltimore, Md: Johns Hopkins University Press, 1935) (1965)

This first, unpublished novel is uncollected in editions of H's work. For its publishing history, see R. L. Purdy (40).

7   THE ORIGINAL MANUSCRIPTS AND PAPERS OF THOMAS HARDY. A COLLECTION ON MICROFILM (Wakefield, Yorkshire: E. P. Microfilm Ltd, 1976)

Eighteen reels of microfilm present many of H's manuscripts. Most of the major novels and poems are included, plus notebooks and the typescript of *The Early Life*. Fascinating publication, but of limited use to the textual scholar, who needs to consult the original manuscripts.

8   Creighton, T. R. M. (ed.)
     POEMS OF THOMAS HARDY: A NEW SELECTION

(London: Macmillan, 1974). Extract from Introduction is reprinted in Gibson and Johnson (eds), A CASEBOOK (429), pp 238–40

Arranges some 280 poems in five mainly thematic groupings (Nature and Man, Love, The Past and the Present, Poems Dramatic and Personative, and Ballads and Narrative Poems). Poems chosen to give a cross-section of H's writing, rather than to present his best or most familiar poems. This is a useful classroom text rather than a scholarly edition. Introduction chiefly describes or justifies principles of selection. Appendices helpfully reprint Prefaces from individual volumes of poems, and H's comments on poetry, almost entirely culled from Florence Hardy's *Life* (58). Notes to the poems are usually factual.

9   Davies, Walford (ed.)
THOMAS HARDY: SELECTED POEMS (London: Dent, 1983)

Sensible introduction. Thematic arrangement of poems not as interesting as Creighton's similar enterprise (8).

10   Gibson, James (ed.)
THE COMPLETE POEMS OF THOMAS HARDY, The New Wessex Edition (London: Macmillan, 1976)

First new edition of H's collected poems since 1930. Includes all previously uncollected poems and fragments. Not an 'academic' edition, but does indicate some of H's revisions. Large type and spacious layout.

11   Gibson, James (ed.)
THE COMPLETE POEMS OF THOMAS HARDY: A VARIORUM EDITION (London: Macmillan, 1979)

A major work of scholarship, showing H's prolific revisions and the many variant readings in editions of the poetry. Gibson is invariably reliable in establishing the text of the poems.

12 Hynes, Samuel (ed.)
THE COMPLETE POETICAL WORKS OF THOMAS
HARDY, 3 vols (London: Oxford University Press,
1982–85)

Excellent and fascinating edition complements James Gibson's Variorum (11). Hynes aims to establish 'a final,
definitive text' and includes all variant readings in manuscript
and printed sources. Fuller annotation on individual poems
than was possible in Gibson.
Vol. 1 includes editorial introduction and the poems and
related sketches in *Wessex Poems, Poems of the Past and the
Present* and *Time's Laughingstocks.*
Vol. 2 comprises the poems in *Satires of Circumstance,
Moments of Vision* and *Late Lyrics and Earlier.*
Vol. 3 contains the poems in *Human Shows* and *Winter
Words,* uncollected poems, appendices and glossaries of
dialect, archaic and obsolete words and of place names.

13 Hynes, Samuel (ed.)
THOMAS HARDY, Oxford Authors (London: Oxford
University Press, 1984)

A selected edition including more than half of H's poems.
This is the largest such selection. Texts are based on those in
Hynes' *Complete Poetical Works* (12), but textual variants
are omitted. Hynes' introduction claims that H's best poems
are his short lyrics which were 'written, as it seems, for
himself alone, to give a private order to his feelings'. H's
verse belongs to that chief English lineage of 'a poetry,
essentially, of normative experience: plain, low-pitched,
physical, and abiding'. The selection, in addition to the very
stimulating introduction, contains helpful notes and relevant
passages from H's other writings.

14 Wilson, Eliane (ed.)
THOMAS HARDY: AN AUTOBIOGRAPHY IN
VERSE, with a biographical study by Howard Shaw,
calligraphy and illustrations by Frederick Marns (London:
Shepheard-Walwyn, 1984)

Beautifully produced selection of eighty poems by H illustrating various stages of his life from childhood to old age. A
unique feature is that the poems are inscribed in very

attractive calligraphy, and Shaw's urbane introduction is reliable and thoughtful. The poems selected tend to depict the gloom-ridden and sombre H.

Non-fictional prose

15   Beatty, C. J. P. (ed.)
THE ARCHITECTURAL NOTEBOOK OF THOMAS HARDY (Dorchester: Dorset Natural History and Archaeological Society; Philadelphia: George S. Macmanus, 1966)

Fascinating reproduction of the notebook which H kept while practising as an architect between 1862 and 1872. Many intricate sketches for church and domestic architecture. Beatty's excellent introduction explains the architectural background and the relevance of H's training for our understanding of such novels as *L* and *JO*.

16   Björk, Lennart A. (ed.)
THE LITERARY NOTEBOOKS OF THOMAS HARDY, 2 vols (London: Macmillan, 1985)

Prints four notebooks in which H copied out or extracted passages from books from the 1870s to 1927. This is a complete edition, superseding and incorporating (with revision) Björk's *Literary Notes* (17). Björk produces a brilliantly annotated edition which identifies the source of almost every entry and discusses the significance of many of them. An indispensable research aid.

17   Björk, Lennart A. (ed.)
THE LITERARY NOTES OF THOMAS HARDY, Gothenburg Studies in English No. 29 (1974) (New York: Humanities Press, 1975)

A scrupulous work of scholarship. This is the first of a projected two-volume edition of H's notebooks and is divided into two parts, Text and Notes, separately bound. The Text transcribes H's commonplace books which contain his observations and quotations from his reading. The Notes identify nearly all of H's sources and discuss the significance of the entries. An outstanding edition. [Superseded by previous item.]

18   Brennecke, Ernest, Jr (ed.)
      LIFE AND ART, BY THOMAS HARDY (New York: Greenberg, 1925)

      Assembles some of H's non-fictional prose. Superseded by Orel's much fuller collection (20).

19   Hardy, Evelyn (ed.)
      THOMAS HARDY'S NOTEBOOKS, AND SOME LETTERS FROM JULIA AUGUSTA MARTIN (London: Hogarth Press, 1955)

      Poorly edited selection of notes from two of H's Memoranda notebooks. Incorporated in Richard H. Taylor's definitive edition of such material (21)
         Julia Augusta Martin was the lady of the manor in H's childhood, and his letters recall this period.

20   Orel, Harold (ed.)
      THOMAS HARDY'S PERSONAL WRITINGS: PREFACES, LITERARY OPINIONS, REMINISCENCES (Lawrence: University of Kansas Press, 1966; London: Macmillan, 1967)

      Valuable collection of H's occasional non-fiction writing. Contains his prefaces to his own and others' works, and a wide selection of other essays, such as 'The Profitable Reading of Fiction', 'Candour in English Fiction', 'The Science of Fiction' and 'The Dorsetshire Labourer'. Supersedes Brennecke's comparable but much narrower selection (18).

21   Taylor, Richard H. (ed.)
      THE PERSONAL NOTEBOOKS OF THOMAS HARDY (London: Macmillan, 1978)

      Four of H's personal notebooks are edited: Memoranda, I; Memoranda, II; Schools of Painting Notebook; Trumpet-Major Notebook. The first two contain H's thoughts and observations over six decades. The third shows H's efforts as an autodidact. The fourth contains background notes on clothing, soldiers and local military life, and shows H's careful research into the world of *TM*. Lengthy appendix reproduces and annotates the unpublished typescript passages which H eventually omitted from his veiled autobiography (58).

A fascinating volume, excellently edited and annotated.

Letters

22   Hardy, Evelyn and Pinion, F. B. (eds)
ONE RARE FAIR WOMAN; THOMAS HARDY'S
LETTERS TO FLORENCE HENNIKER 1893–1922 (Coral
Gables: University of Miami Press, 1972)

153 letters from H to Mrs Henniker illustrate their relationship, at times intense, over many years. The editors helpfully correlate the letters with H's poems about her. This is the most interesting of the thematic selections of letters.

23   Purdy, Richard Little and Millgate, Michael (eds)
THE COLLECTED LETTERS OF THOMAS HARDY
Vol. 1 1840–1892 (Oxford: The Clarendon Press; New
York: Oxford University Press, 1978), Vol. 2 1893–1901
(Oxford: The Clarendon Press; New York: Oxford
University Press, 1980), Vol. 3 1902–1908 (Oxford: The
Clarendon Press; New York: Oxford University Press,
1982), Vol. 4 1909–1913 (Oxford: The Clarendon Press;
New York: Oxford University Press, 1984), Vol. 5
1914–1919 (Oxford: The Clarendon Press; New York:
Oxford University Press, 1985), Vol. 6 1920–1925 (Oxford:
The Clarendon Press; New York: Oxford University Press,
1987), Vol. 7 1926–1927 (Oxford: The Clarendon Press;
New York: Oxford University Press, 1988)

The definitive edition of the letters. Exemplary editing and annotation. Two more volumes published in 1988. Vol. 1 contains a General Introduction. Each volume has an index of recipients. Vol. 7 contains a General Index to the entire edition.

24 Weber, Carl J. (ed.)
'DEAREST EMMIE': THOMAS HARDY'S LETTERS
TO HIS FIRST WIFE (London: Macmillan; New York:
St Martin's Press, 1963)

Useful grouping of seventy-four letters, written to Emma
between 1885 and 1911. Copious annotation.

25 Weber, Carl J. (ed.)
THE LETTERS OF THOMAS HARDY, TRANSCRIBED
FROM THE ORIGINAL AUTOGRAPHS NOW IN THE
COLBY COLLEGE LIBRARY (Waterville, Maine: Colby
College Press, 1954) (1970)

Slightly more than 100 letters, written between 1873 and
1927. Extensive annotation.

26 Weber, Carl J. and Weber, Clara Carter
THOMAS HARDY'S CORRESPONDENCE AT MAX
GATE: A DESCRIPTIVE CHECK LIST (Waterville,
Maine: Colby College Press, 1968)

Lists 854 letters written by H, which are all published in the
collected edition of the letters, edited by Purdy and Millgate
(23). The Webers' compilation will remain of interest for its
catalogue of more than 4,000 letters to H from a wide variety
of correspondents. (Max Gate was H's Dorchester home.)

Bibliographies and surveys of criticism

27 Alexander, B. J.
'Criticism of Thomas Hardy's Novels: A Selected Checklist',
Studies in the Novel 4:4 (Winter 1972) 630–54

Supplements Beebe et al.'s bibliography (29). Covers period
from 1960–72. Same format as Beebe: unannotated listing of
general books and novel-by-novel.

28 Bailey, J. O.
'Changing Fashions in Hardy Scholarship', THOMAS
HARDY AND THE MODERN WORLD (104) 140–54

Largely descriptive survey of criticism on H, grouping
comment by subject matter.

29   Beebe, Maurice, Culotta, Bonnie and Marcus, Erin
      'Criticism of Thomas Hardy: A Selected Checklist', *Modern
      Fiction Studies* 6 (Autumn 1960) 258–79

      A first-class bibliography emphasising post-1940 criticism. In
      three parts; the first two concern general studies and the
      poetry, while the third details studies of individual works of
      fiction. Hardly anything of significance is omitted.

30   Buckler, William E.
      '"In the Seventies": A Centennial Assessment of the
      Unlocking of Thomas Hardy's Vision', *Dickens Studies
      Annual: Essays on Victorian Fiction* 9, ed. Michael Timko,
      Fred Kaplan and Edward Guiliano (New York: AMS Press,
      1981) 233–63

      A spiky, combative and generally dismissive survey of H
      criticism in the 1970s which, he believes, looks rather 'busier'
      than 'inspired'. This is a stimulating, provocative and occa-
      sionally pretentious essay for the experienced scholar.

31   Carter, Kenneth and Whetherly, June M. (eds)
      THOMAS HARDY CATALOGUE: A LIST OF THE
      BOOKS BY AND ABOUT THOMAS HARDY, O.M.
      (1840–1928) IN DORSET COUNTY LIBRARY (1968; 2nd
      edition, Dorchester: Dorset County Library, 1973)

      Catalogues material on H in the library (*not* the museum) at
      Dorchester. Limited in aims but indispensable guide to the
      Hardy collection. Lists editions, translations, criticism, etc.

32   Dunn, Richard J.
      THE ENGLISH NOVEL: TWENTIETH-CENTURY
      CRITICISM, Vol. 1, DEFOE THROUGH HARDY
      (Chicago: Swallow Press, 1976) 88–100

      Unannotated, useful listing of general studies. Begins with a
      novel-by-novel list of criticism.

33   Fayen, George S., Jr
      'Thomas Hardy', VICTORIAN FICTION: A GUIDE TO

RESEARCH, ed. Lionel Stevenson (Cambridge, Mass.: Harvard University Press, 1964) 349–87

Very useful. Surveys in essay-form all aspects of criticism on H up to 1962. Michael Millgate (37) is a sequel to Fayen.

34 Gerber, Helmut E. and Davis, W. Eugene (eds)
THOMAS HARDY: AN ANNOTATED
BIBLIOGRAPHY OF WRITINGS ABOUT HIM (De
Kalb, Illinois: Northern Illinois University Press, 1973)

Invaluable scholarly guide to criticism of H's work. Covers the years 1871–1969. More than 3,000 items in eleven languages are annotated. Includes reviews, biographies, critical books, articles, theses, etc. Attempts definitive coverage of clearly important writings on H. Full annotation of entries, with occasional critical comments. Chronological format gives clear idea of critical developments and fashions, but may hinder the student seeking information on a particular topic or text.

35 Gerber, Helmut E. and Davis, W. Eugene (eds)
THOMAS HARDY: AN ANNOTATED
BIBLIOGRAPHY OF WRITINGS ABOUT HIM, Vol. II
1970–1978 AND SUPPLEMENT FOR 1871–1969 (De Kalb,
Illinois: Northern Illinois University Press, 1983)

Sequel to the previous item. Annotates 1,400 new critical writings on H in period 1970–1978. Supplement gives over 1,200 items from earlier period not included in first volume. Same format and range of coverage. Again, indispensable.

36 Johnson, H. A. T.
THOMAS HARDY 1874–1974: AN ANNOTATED
READING LIST (Manchester: Mather College, 1974)

Selective bibliography in six sections: 1. Works by H; 2. Biography, Letters, etc.; 3. Critical works on H; 4. Critical works with substantial reference to H; 5. Articles in periodicals about H; 6. Background material (history, folklore, topography, etc.).

37   Millgate, Michael
'Thomas Hardy', VICTORIAN FICTION: A SECOND
GUIDE TO RESEARCH, ed. George H. Ford (New York:
Modern Language Association, 1978) 308–32

A lively and readable survey evaluating, in essay-form,
criticism of H's fiction over a twelve-year period, 1963–74.
Sections on bibliography, editions and texts, biography,
general criticism (books, articles and chapters of books) and
studies of individual works and other fiction. A few
comments on criticism of *D*. Very useful reference guide.

38   Pettit, Charles P. C. (ed.)
A CATALOGUE OF THE WORKS OF THOMAS
HARDY (1840–1928) IN DORCHESTER REFERENCE
LIBRARY (Dorchester: Dorset County Library, 1984)

Direct successor to the catalogues by Carter and Whetherly
(31). Catalogues all books on the shelves of the Hardy
Collection. Excludes articles, etc. in the filing cabinets, with
a few exceptions. More specialised than the Carter and
Whetherly catalogues, since it is devoted more to primary
material. Listing completed in November 1983.

39   Pinion, F. B.
'Hardy: 1840–1928', THE ENGLISH NOVEL; SELECT
BIBLIOGRAPHICAL GUIDES, ed. A. E. Dyson
(London: Oxford University Press, 1974) 264–79

Intended as an introduction to criticism of H for the serious
student. Very selective listing of editions, critical works,
biographies, background readings, each followed by succinct
comments.

40   Purdy, Richard Little
THOMAS HARDY: A BIBLIOGRAPHICAL STUDY
(London, New York, Toronto: Oxford University Press,
1954) (1968)

Indispensable and definitive bibliography. Lists first and
collected editions, and uncollected contributions to books,
periodicals and newspapers. Gives details of the composition

of all H's works. Locates manuscripts. Much important biographical information.

41 Stevenson, Lionel
'Thomas Hardy', THE VICTORIAN POETS, ed. Frederic E. Faverty (Cambridge, Mass.: Harvard University Press, 1956) 238–41

Discusses in essay-form the biographies and bibliographies, but mostly devoted to criticism of poetry. Brief but useful.

42 Taylor, Richard H.
'A Survey of Recent Hardy Studies', THOMAS HARDY ANNUAL No. 1, ed. Norman Page (London: Macmillan, 1982) 152–71

Invaluable descriptive account of the major critical activity between 1978 and 1981. Six sections examine 'Editions', 'Textual Studies', 'Bibliographies and handbooks', 'Biography, letters and notebooks', 'Critical studies: novels and stories', and 'Critical studies: poetry'. Followed by 'A Hardy Bibliography, 1978–81' 190–205, which gives an extensive listing of criticism.

43 Taylor, Richard H.
'A Survey of Recent Hardy Studies', THOMAS HARDY ANNUAL No. 2, ed. Norman Page (London: Macmillan, 1984) 196–214

Survey in essay-form of recent criticism, followed by 'A Hardy Bibliography, 1981–82' 255–61, which lists such material.

44 Taylor, Richard H.
'A Survey of Recent Hardy Studies', THOMAS HARDY ANNUAL No. 3, ed. Norman Page (London: Macmillan, 1985) 129–43

Annotated review-essay of the year's criticism, in same format as previous volumes. Followed by a more complete list, with full bibliographic details, in Taylor's 'A Hardy Bibliography, 1982–83' 184–9.

45   Taylor, Richard H.
'A Survey of Recent Hardy Studies', THOMAS HARDY
ANNUAL No. 4, ed. Norman Page (London: Macmillan,
1986) 165–85

Descriptive survey in essay form, followed by a listing of
criticism in 'A Hardy Bibliography, 1983–84' 206–9.

46   Taylor, Richard H.
'A Survey of Recent Hardy Studies', THOMAS HARDY
ANNUAL No. 5, ed. Norman Page (London: Macmillan,
1987) 157–81

Annotated bibliographical survey, in same format as previous
volumes. Followed by 'A Hardy Bibliography, 1984–85'
212–17, which lists criticism.

47   Taylor, Richard H.
'Thomas Hardy: A Reader's Guide', THOMAS HARDY:
THE WRITER AND HIS BACKGROUND, ed. Norman
Page (London: Bell & Hyman, 1980) 219–58

Excellent survey in essay-form of H's critical reputation,
noting the landmarks in criticism of H and the varying ways
in which his fiction and poetry have been viewed during this
century. The essay is followed by 'Thomas Hardy: A Select
Bibliography' 259–72, which helpfully lists the works discussed earlier under a number of headings (e.g. Studies of
specific works, Critical studies of the poetry).

48   Weber, Carl J.
THE FIRST HUNDRED YEARS OF THOMAS HARDY
1840–1940: A CENTENARY BIBLIOGRAPHY OF
HARDIANA (Waterville, Maine: Colby College Library,
1940)

The first important bibliography of criticism about H. Extensive, but without annotation. Now superseded by the two
volumes of bibliography edited by Gerber and Davis (34–5).

Biography and Biographical Material

49   Barber, D. F. (ed.)
      CONCERNING THOMAS HARDY: A COMPOSITE
      PORTRAIT FROM MEMORY (London: Charles Skilton,
      1968)

      Synthesises the first forty-two monographs on H's life in
      Cox's series (51). Barber organises the material under
      various headings, e.g. 'Love and Thomas Hardy', 'The social
      celebrity'.

50   Brennecke, Ernest, Jr
      THE LIFE OF THOMAS HARDY (New York:
      Greenberg, 1925)

      The first book-length biography, disliked by H for its
      'impertinence'.

51   Cox, J. Stevens (ed.)
      THOMAS HARDY: MATERIALS FOR A STUDY OF
      HIS LIFE, TIMES AND WORKS, Monographs 1–35
      (Mount Durand, St Peter Port, Guernsey: Toucan Press,
      1968); Vol. 2 THOMAS HARDY: MORE MATERIALS
      FOR A STUDY OF HIS LIFE, TIMES AND WORKS,
      Monographs 36–72 (Mount Durand, St Peter Port,
      Guernsey: Toucan Press, 1971)

      Collection of monographs published 1962–1971. Many of
      them are gossip and tittle-tattle (H as remembered by his
      barber, cook and cleaner), but some are scholarly contribu-
      tions to biography. Espouses Lois Deacon's speculative view
      of H's relationship with Tryphena Sparks (see 52). Influential
      in its cumulative impression of H as an unpleasant little man,
      certainly not a hero to his valet.

52   Deacon, Lois and Coleman, Terry
      PROVIDENCE AND MR. HARDY (London: Hutchinson,
      1966)

Proposes that H fathered a son, Randal, by his cousin, Tryphena Sparks, in 1868. The 'evidence' for this is largely fanciful and conjectural. The myth is demolished by Robert Gittings in an appendix to *Young Thomas Hardy* (54).

53   Doheny, John R.
'The Youth of Thomas Hardy', *Thomas Hardy Year Book* 12 (1984) 6–115

Rather speculative survey of H's youth and adolescence, centring on his love affairs. Supports the view that H had a sexual relationship with Tryphena Sparks.

54   Gittings, Robert
YOUNG THOMAS HARDY (1975) and THE OLDER HARDY (London: Heinemann Educational, 1978)

The second volume was published in the United States as THOMAS HARDY'S LATER YEARS (Boston: Little, Brown, 1978)

Serious and original research, and extremely readable. Consistent view of H as a 'tragi-comic contrast between mean and noble', eternally adolescent and horribly flawed. This partial and biased view nevertheless produces a number of new insights of great value. A challenging, exciting, iconoclastic biography.

55   Gittings, Robert and Manton, Jo
THE SECOND MRS HARDY (London: Heinemann; Seattle: University of Washington Press, 1979)

Very readable biography of Florence Dugdale, whom H married in 1914. Essential for our understanding of the later part of H's life.

56   Hardy, Evelyn
THOMAS HARDY: A CRITICAL BIOGRAPHY
(London: Hogarth Press; New York: St Martin's Press, 1954)

Rather simplistic biography in places. Traces some patterns of imagery quite well.

57   Hardy, Evelyn and Gittings, Robert (eds)
       SOME RECOLLECTIONS BY EMMA HARDY WITH
       NOTES BY EVELYN HARDY TOGETHER WITH
       SOME RELEVANT POEMS BY THOMAS HARDY
       WITH NOTES BY ROBERT GITTINGS (London and
       New York: Oxford University Press, 1961)

H's first wife completed *Some Recollections* in 1911, the year
before her death. She describes her childhood, family background and H's courtship. These charming and moving brief
reminiscences, though occasionally sentimental, elicit much
sympathy for her. Fourteen poems are appended to show the
influence of Emma's recollections on H's writing after her
death.

58   Hardy, Florence Emily
       THE EARLY LIFE OF THOMAS HARDY, 1840–1891
       (London and New York: Macmillan, 1928), reissued with
       THE LATER YEARS OF THOMAS HARDY, 1892–1928
       (1930) in 2 vols (London and New York: Macmillan, 1933).
       Two vols reprinted in one as THE LIFE OF THOMAS
       HARDY, 1840–1928 (London: Macmillan; New York:
       St Martin's Press, 1962)

In spite of being presented as if they were biographies by H's
second wife, these volumes are essentially H's autobio-
graphies dictated to Florence in the third person and
published posthumously. An invaluable source of primary
information. See also Michael Millgate's revision of *The Life*
(61).

59   Holland, Clive
       THOMAS HARDY, O.M.: THE MAN, HIS WORKS,
       AND THE LAND OF WESSEX (London: Jenkins, 1933)

Early biography. Conventional account drawing heavily on
the *Life* (58).

60   Kay-Robinson, Denys
       THE FIRST MRS THOMAS HARDY (London:
       Macmillan, 1979)

Sympathetic biography of Emma Hardy, who no longer
appears as the villain of tradition. Her marriage to H

foundered on misunderstandings and repressed love, and H's response to her death in his poetry shows the release, rather than the revival, of his feelings for her.

61   Millgate, Michael (ed.)
THE LIFE AND WORK OF THOMAS HARDY BY
THOMAS HARDY (London: Macmillan, 1985)

Revised edition of Florence Hardy's *Early Life* and *Later Years* (58), which is mostly by H himself. Millgate has restored what H originally wrote, excising the additions and revisions which his wife made after his death. Most of the omitted passages are listed in an appendix. Also has excellent new biographical index.

H 'emerges less attractively' in this new edition. There are many references now to aristocrats he met, and his ferocious response to reviews is no longer censored. There are also many more references to his first wife.

62   Millgate, Michael
THOMAS HARDY: A BIOGRAPHY (London: Oxford
University Press, 1982)

The most balanced and objective biography to date. Thorough scholarship and reasonable, judicious attitude to his subject. Defends H against some of the baser charges against his personality, albeit at the expense of his wives, especially Emma.

63   Orel, Harold
THE FINAL YEARS OF THOMAS HARDY, 1912–1928
(London: Macmillan; Lawrence, Kansas: University Press of
Kansas, 1976)

Studies late life and work of H, after death of first wife. Chapters on Emma Hardy, occasional poems, Nature, drama, Christianity, war and H's reflections on history. Many of the later poems are far from pessimistic in tone.

64   Orel, Harold
'Hardy, Kipling and Haggard', *English Literature in
Transition* 25 (1982) 232–48

Mainly biographical essay linking the three writers. One of Kipling's characters is based on H. Little direct literary influence, though.

65 Orel, Harold
'The Literary Friendships of Thomas Hardy', *English Literature in Transition* 24:3 (1981) 131–45

Traces H's lasting friendship with six authors: William Barnes, Horace Moule, George Meredith, A. C. Swinburne, Leslie Stephen and Edmund Gosse. An antidote to the view of H as secretive misanthrope.

66 O'Sullivan, Timothy
THOMAS HARDY: AN ILLUSTRATED BIOGRAPHY (London: Macmillan, 1975)

This excellently illustrated and reliable account of H's life is a pleasure to read.

67 Rutland, William R.
THOMAS HARDY: A STUDY OF HIS WRITINGS AND THEIR BACKGROUND (Oxford: Basil Blackwell, 1938)

The first major biography. Opening three chapters discuss the intellectual background to the works and especially the influence of H's reading in the classics and the Bible. Later gives chronological discussions of the novels and poems. Still valuable in its emphasis on H's intellectual development.

68 Taylor, Richard H. (ed.)
EMMA HARDY DIARIES (Ashington: Mid-Northumberland Arts Groups; Manchester: Carcanet New Press, 1985)

Very attractive edition of the diaries of H's first wife. Mainly a record of continental tours. Interesting glimpses of H and the growing marital estrangement. Reproduced in facsimile with a transcription in print.

69   Weber, Carl J.
      HARDY AND THE LADY FROM MADISON SQUARE
      (Waterville, Maine: Colby College Press, 1952)

      Examines H's long friendship with Rebekah Owen, an
      American living in England who was an ardent but tedious
      devotee of H's work. Interesting recollections by Miss Owen.

70   Weber, Carl J.
      HARDY OF WESSEX: HIS LIFE AND LITERARY
      CAREER (New York: Columbia University Press; London:
      Routledge & Kegan Paul, 1940; revised edition 1965)

      A biographical rather than a critical study which runs an
      account of Hardy's life *pari passu* with a commentary on his
      writings. Weber emphasises the extent to which H was ready
      'to use for fictional purposes his own and his wife's experi-
      ence in real life'. *JO* is seen as the most autobiographical of
      the novels. Full attention is given to publishing history and
      critical reception, both in England and America, and there is
      some comment on *D* and the poems, particularly those of
      1912–13 on Emma. Pages 299–304 give brief factual accounts
      of all the short stories. As biography this is now largely
      superseded by Gittings (54) and Millgate (62), but it is still a
      readable and informative, if slightly pious, account of H's
      career.
          The 2nd edition is not significantly revised and omits many
      of the 1st edition's valuable appendices.

71   Woolf, Virginia
      A WRITER'S DIARY: BEING EXTRACTS FROM THE
      DIARY OF VIRGINIA WOOLF, ed. Leonard Woolf
      (London: Hogarth Press, 1952; New York: Harcourt, Brace,
      1954)

      Interesting account of a visit to H in July 1926. Literature
      'seemed to him an amusement, far away too, scarcely to be
      taken seriously'. Woolf seems surprised that H showed 'no
      trace to my thinking of the simple peasant'. H's recorded
      comments are insignificant, but Woolf gives a factual and
      sympathetic portrait of the elderly H at home, very much the
      '"Great Victorian"'.

Background Material

72 Beningfield, Gordon
    HARDY COUNTRY (London: Allen Lane, 1983)

    Beautiful colour drawings accompany Anthea Zeman's lucid
    text. Excellently produced and pleasurable work.

73 Brasnett, Hugh
    THOMAS HARDY: A PICTORIAL GUIDE (Romney
    Marsh: John Waite, 1984)

    Attractive collection of photographs of places depicted by H,
    with accompanying text. Enthusiastic commentary and useful
    maps.

74 Fowles, John and Draper, Jo
    THOMAS HARDY'S ENGLAND (London: Cape, 1984)

    Reproduces sepia photographs of Wessex during H's lifetime.
    Introduced and edited by Fowles, who emphasises the
    fascination of a lost world and the transformation of England
    in the nineteenth century from a predominantly rural to a
    predominantly urban country. Draper's commentary shows
    how the pictorial record of rural life depicts the raw material
    of H's work.

75 Hawkins, Desmond
    HARDY'S WESSEX (London: Macmillan, 1983)

    Highly recommended topography. Some excellent photo-
    graphs of Wessex, some in colour. Concentrates on areas
    such as Egdon Heath, Mellstock and Lyonnesse which
    'vitalized Hardy's imagination'.

76 Hurst, Alan
    THOMAS HARDY: AN ILLUSTRATED DICTIONARY
    (London: Kaye & Ward, 1980)

Useful handbook, similar but inferior to Pinion's companion (83). Gives alphabetical dictionary, notes on Wessex, locations of characters and survey of dramatisations. A reliable source of basic information attractively presented. Many photographs.

77   Kay-Robinson, Denys
HARDY'S WESSEX REAPPRAISED (New York:
St Martin's Press, 1971; Newton Abbot: David and Charles 1972)

Topographical study identifies 'originals' of buildings and places of H's fictional Wessex. Used with suitable caution, this is an enterprising work. Sectional organisation with photographs, maps and sketches. Refers to most titles, and supersedes previous such handbooks. [See next item.]

78   Kay-Robinson, Denys
THE LANDSCAPE OF THOMAS HARDY (Exeter:
Webb & Bower, 1984)

This topographical study is a revised and updated version of Kay-Robinson's *Hardy's Wessex Reappraised* (77). Identifies locations but carefully distinguishes between fact and fiction, bricks and books. Invaluable guide, with many new photographs by Simon McBride.

79   Kerr, Barbara
BOUND TO THE SOIL: A SOCIAL HISTORY OF
DORSET 1750–1918 (London: John Baker, 1968)

Though it does not discuss H, this provides one of the best local-historical studies of nineteenth-century Dorset. Its chapters on copyholding, on the woodland economy, on the Dorchester corn trade and the impact of outside mechanised contractors supply suggestive and well-documented contexts for the world of *MC* and *W* especially.

80   Lea, Hermann
A HANDBOOK TO THE WESSEX COUNTRY OF
MR. THOMAS HARDY'S NOVELS AND POEMS
(London: Kegan Paul, Trench, Trubner [1905]) (1906)

Reliable guide to Wessex, with sketches and maps. Lea was assisted by H, who 'never admitted more than that the places named fictitiously were *suggested* by such and such a real place'.

81 Lea, Hermann
THOMAS HARDY'S WESSEX (London: Macmillan, 1913)

Identifies the real places to which the fictional settings in H's work are said to correspond. Acknowledges that 'the exact Wessex of the books exists nowhere outside them'.

82 Leeming, Glenda
WHO'S WHO IN THOMAS HARDY (London: Elm Tree Books; New York: Taplinger Publishing Co., 1975)

Lists and describes all characters and named animals in H's novels. Omits short stories.

83 Pinion, F.B.
A HARDY COMPANION: A GUIDE TO THE WORKS OF THOMAS HARDY AND THEIR BACKGROUND (London: Macmillan; New York: St Martin's Press, 1968)

An invaluable handbook. Four chapters on novels, stories, plays and poems give details of their composition, publication and reception. Five chapters on special problems or preoccupations in H's work: The Wessex tradition; Views on art, tragedy, and fiction; Aspects of the unusual and irrational; Towards symbolism; Christianity, scientific philosophy, and politics. One chapter on influences and recollections, especially good on H's interest in architecture, music, painting and literature. A useful section of 300 pages entitled 'Dictionary of people and places in Hardy's works'. Ends with a glossary of H's vocabulary (dialect, archaic, Shakespearean and foreign words).

84 *Quarterly Review* 3, no. 222 (1862) 218–318

Anonymous review provides a contemporary picture of Dorset, its social, agricultural and economic condition. One of the best contemporary descriptions of 'Wessex' (probably written by a friend of H, one of the Moules).

85   Saxelby, F. Outwin
A THOMAS HARDY DICTIONARY: THE CHARACTERS AND SCENES OF THE NOVELS AND POEMS ALPHABETICALLY ARRANGED AND DESCRIBED (London: Routledge & Kegan Paul; New York: Dutton, 1911)

Gives synopses of plots and lists of place names. Dictionary identifies references in H's work.

Collections of Essays

86   Butler, Lance St John (ed.)
THOMAS HARDY AFTER FIFTY YEARS (London:
Macmillan, 1977)

Collection of original essays annotated individually, by the
following: F. B. Pinion (591), R. M. Rehder (592), John
Fowles (399), Robert Gittings (485), Michael Alexander
(457), T. R. M. Creighton (622), David Lodge (587), Mark
Kinkead-Weekes (636), Michael Irwin and Ian Gregor (650),
Lance St John Butler (624), F. E. Halliday (700) and R. C.
Schweik (606).

87   *Cahiers Victoriens & Edouardiens* [Special Issue: *Studies in
Thomas Hardy,* ed. Annie Escuret] 12 (1980) (Montpellier:
Université Paul Valéry, 1980)

Collection of eleven original articles, mostly in English.
Pierre Coustillas, 'Gissing on Hardy: A Novelist's View of a
Contemporary Writer', pp 1–18.
Simon Gatrell, 'Hardy and the Critics', pp 19–44.
F. B. Pinion, 'Hardy's Literary Imagination', pp 45–56.
Gregory Stevens Cox, *'The Mumming Play of St George',*
pp 57–72.
J. Sénéchal-Teissedou, 'Focalisation, regard et désir dans *Far
from the Madding Crowd',* pp 73–83.
Annie Escuret, '"Tess des d'Urbervilles": le corps et le
signe', pp 85–136.
Jean R. Brooks, *'The Dynasts* as Total Theatre', pp 137–78.
Jean Vaché, 'Structures métaphoriques dans "Les
Dynastes"', pp 179–99.
Robert M. Rehder, 'Hardy's Lyrics: Visions of Moments', pp
201–10.
Lance St John Butler, 'Hardy's Tragedy of *The Queen of
Cornwall',* pp 211–18.
Michael Alexander, 'Better Than Beer, More Lasting Than
Bronze', pp 219–26 (review article).

88   Cox, R. G. (ed.)
THOMAS HARDY: THE CRITICAL HERITAGE
(London: Routledge & Kegan Paul; New York: Barnes &
Noble, 1970)

The most important anthology of contemporary reviews. Assembles more than seventy-five essays on most of H's novels and volumes of poetry in a balanced survey of his critical reception. H clearly attracted a good deal of thoughtful and sympathetic appreciation.

89   Drabble, Margaret (ed.)
THE GENIUS OF THOMAS HARDY (London: Weidenfeld & Nicolson, 1976)

Collection of sixteen original essays by different distinguished critics and writers, such as Sir John Betjeman, Geoffrey Grigson and Lord David Cecil. Divided into three sections: 'The life', 'The work' (including essays on *T, JO* and the poetry) and 'The genius of Thomas Hardy' (exploring rather predictable areas such as H's interest in philosophy, architecture, history and the natural world). A traditional, familiar and competent introduction to H.

90   Draper, Ronald Philip (ed.)
HARDY; THE TRAGIC NOVELS: *THE RETURN OF THE NATIVE, THE MAYOR OF CASTERBRIDGE, TESS OF THE D'URBERVILLES, JUDE THE OBSCURE:* A CASEBOOK (London: Macmillan, 1975)

Studies of H's tragic novels in a collection of critical essays and extracts. The Introduction summarises the publication and reception of these novels and comments on the poetic and more sociological approaches to H's work.

Part One: Comments by H.
Part Two: Early and more recent comments (including Lionel Johnson, D. H. Lawrence, Virginia Woolf and Raymond Williams).
Part Three: Modern studies on individual novels

   (i) *RN:* Reprints John Paterson (225), and Leonard W. Deen (207)
   (ii) *MC:* Robert Schweik (256) and J. C. Maxwell (251)
   (iii) *T:* Douglas Brown (117), David Lodge (308) and Tony Tanner (316)
   (iv) *JO:* Robert B. Heilman (341) and Ian Gregor (129).

Concludes with select bibliography.

91 Draper, Ronald Philip (ed.)
THOMAS HARDY; THREE PASTORAL NOVELS:
*UNDER THE GREENWOOD TREE, FAR FROM THE
MADDING CROWD, THE WOODLANDERS:* A
CASEBOOK (London: Macmillan, 1987)

Studies of H's three novels in the established format of the
Casebook series. The Introduction surveys the novels' reception and critical history, and discusses H's particular version
of pastoral.

Part One: Comments by H (Prefaces from editions of the
novels and relevant extracts from the *Life*).
Part Two: Reviews and Early Criticism. (Includes comments by Henry James, Virginia Woolf, J. M.
Barrie, Horace Moule and others).
Part Three: Modern Studies on Individual Novels (extracts
from recent criticism).

UGT: Reprints John F. Danby (170), Michael
M. Millgate (148), Norman Page (176)
and Peter J. Casagrande (121)
FMC: Reprints Roy Morrell (149), John Lucas
(670), Alan Shelston (196) and Andrew
Enstice (127)
W: Reprints Douglas Brown (117), Merryn
Williams (167), Michael Squires (678)
and Shelagh Hunter (676).

Concludes with select bibliography.

92 *English* 22 (Summer 1973)

Special Hardy number. Contents annotated separately: see
Shalom Rachman (359), Robert A. Draffan (171) and K. W.
Salter (643).

93 Guerard, Albert J. (ed.)
HARDY: A COLLECTION OF CRITICAL ESSAYS
(Englewood Cliffs, NJ: Prentice Hall, 1963)

Reprints articles by or extracts from the work of Donald
Davidson (576), Morton D. Zabel (600), D. H. Lawrence
(144), John Holloway (701), Albert Guerard (131), Dorothy

Van Ghent (319), John Paterson (253), A. Alvarez (323),
Delmore Schwartz (529), W. H. Auden (460), David Perkins
(518) and Samuel Hynes (430).
Editor's Introduction and Selected Bibliography.

94   *Inscape Critical Series* [Special Issue, *Thomas Hardy,* ed.
David R. Shore and Keith G. Wilson] 16 (1980) (Ottawa:
University of Ottawa Press, 1980)

Includes articles by Stephen W. Canham (on love and
passion in the novels), Ernest L. Fontana (on *Moments of
Vision*), Janet B. Wright (*JO* and the fiction of the New
Woman), Marlene Springer (the use of allusion in *RN*) and
Kristin Brady (on 'The Fiddler of the Reels').

95   Kramer, Dale (ed.)
CRITICAL APPROACHES TO THE FICTION OF
THOMAS HARDY (London: Macmillan, 1979)

Excellent collection of original essays, demonstrating the
range of recent approaches to H's novels, including formalist,
feminist, structuralist and psychological readings.
    The following authors are included (for annotation, refer
to the entry numbered in parentheses): Dale Kramer (705),
Daniel R. Schwarz (593), W. J. Keith (651), Peter J.
Casagrande (182), Simon Gatrell (186), Elaine Showalter
(257), Mary Jacobus (274), Leon Waldoff (320), Richard C.
Carpenter (409), Michael Ryan (402), David Lodge (352)
and James R. Kincaid (585).

96   Lerner, Laurence and Holmstrom, John (eds)
THOMAS HARDY AND HIS READERS: A
SELECTION OF CONTEMPORARY REVIEWS
(London: Bodley Head; New York: Barnes & Noble, 1968)

Miscellany of reviews, chiefly of H's major novels. Not as
balanced or representative as R. G. Cox's comparable
edition (88).

97   Page, Norman (ed.)
THOMAS HARDY ANNUAL No. 1 (London: Macmillan,
1982)

Contains original articles by the following authors, annotated separately: Peter J. Casagrande (686), Arthur Pollard (671), Merryn Williams (365), John Bayley (395), Rosemary Sumner (397), Tom Paulin (515), Peter W. Coxon (690), Lennart A. Björk (657), John Lucas (503) and Richard H. Taylor (42). Plus Editor's introduction, a poem on H by Christopher Wiseman, and 'Three Unpublished Letters by John Addington Symonds' to H. Reviews.

98   Page, Norman (ed.)
       THOMAS HARDY ANNUAL No. 2 (London: Macmillan, 1984)

Contains original articles, by the following authors, annotated separately: Simon Gatrell (411), Lawrence Jones (703), J. T. Laird (637), Frank R. Giordano, Jr (270), Glenn Irvin (273), Arlene M. Jackson (661), Peter J. Casagrande (441), Norman Arkans (458), Ian Gregor and Michael Irwin (645), Timothy Hands (172), Lloyd Siemens (714), Annie Escuret (695) and Richard H. Taylor (43). Also contains editor's introduction and reviews.

99   Page, Norman (ed.)
       THOMAS HARDY ANNUAL No. 3 (London: Macmillan, 1985)

A collection of original articles, annotated separately, by the following authors: Joan Grundy (634), Robert Langbaum (638), Rosemary Sumner (597), Michael Rabiger (312), J. B. Smith (419), Norman Page (588), Bryn Caless (685) and Richard H. Taylor (44).
    Also includes editor's introduction, reviews, and Samir Elbarbary's '*Tess* and Joyce's *Portrait*: a Possible Parallel' 74–8.

100   Page, Norman (ed.)
       THOMAS HARDY ANNUAL No. 4 (London: Macmillan, 1986)

Original essays by B. E. Maidment (662), Harold Orel (570), Peter Widdowson (654), Simon Gatrell (367), Fred Reid (193), Kristin Brady (284), F. B. Pinion (358) and Richard H. Taylor (45). Also includes editor's introduction and reviews.

101   Page, Norman (ed.)
THOMAS HARDY ANNUAL No. 5 (London: Macmillan, 1987)

A collection of original articles, annotated separately, by the following authors: John Bayley (263), Dale Kramer (604), Lesley Higgins (272), Lionel Adey (178), Fran E. Chalfont (183), George Wing (422), Samuel Hynes (582), Norman Page (589), Rosemarie Morgan (646) and Richard H. Taylor (46).

Also includes editor's introduction, reviews, and Keith Wilson's 'A Note on the Provenance of folio 9 of "Saturday Night in Arcady"' 182–4.

102   Page, Norman (ed.)
THOMAS HARDY: THE WRITER AND HIS BACKGROUND (London: Bell & Hyman, 1980)

Collection of nine original articles by distinguished scholars, mostly on rather predictable topics. Valuable and sound background work.

Articles by the following authors, annotated individually: Merryn and Raymond Williams (674), Philip Collins (689), George Wing (656), Lennart A. Björk (658), Roger Robinson (571), Norman Page (611), Samuel Hynes (492), James Gibson (603) and Richard H. Taylor (47).

103   Pinion, F. B. (ed.)
BUDMOUTH ESSAYS ON THOMAS HARDY: PAPERS PRESENTED AT THE 1975 SUMMER SCHOOL (Dorchester: Thomas Hardy Society, 1976)

Contains original articles by the following authors, annotated separately: Desmond Hawkins (581), Robert C. Schweik (195), H. A. T. Johnson (388), Roy Morrell (369), Maire A. Quinn (417), Lennart A. Björk (325), Melvyn Bragg (327), F. B. Pinion (712), John Paterson (667), Walter F. Wright (632), Frank R. Giordano (483), Harold Orel (510), Tom Paulin (514) and Keith Wilson (542).

104   Pinion, F. B. (ed.)
THOMAS HARDY AND THE MODERN WORLD: PAPERS PRESENTED AT THE 1973 SUMMER

SCHOOL (Dorchester, Dorset: Thomas Hardy Society Ltd, 1974)

Articles by the following authors are annotated separately: J. O. Bailey (28, 680), C. J. P. Beatty (180), F. R. Southerington (231), F. B. Pinion (630), Harold Orel (511), Lord David Cecil (469) and James Gibson (481).
Contains versions of chapters in the books on H by Jean R. Brooks (116) and Robert Gittings (54)
   Also publishes Desmond Hawkins' 'Thomas Hardy and Radio', 60–70.

105   Smith, Anne (ed.)
      THE NOVELS OF THOMAS HARDY (London: Vision Press, 1979)

A volume of nine original essays demonstrating the 'variety of reading experience' which H's major novels offer.
   Essays, individually annotated, by the following authors: Andrew Enstice (694), Rosalind Miles (618), Barbara Hardy (173), Robert B. Heilman (217), Juliet M. Grindle (241), Rosemary L. Eakins (290), Patricia Gallivan (335), Philippa Tristram (718) and Simon Gatrell (602).

106   *Southern Review,* Thomas Hardy Centennial Edition 6
      (Summer 1940)

A landmark in H studies for the prominence it gives to the poetry; eight of the fourteen substantial and original essays discuss the verse.
   A collection of articles, annotated separately, by W. H. Auden (460), Howard Baker (462), Jacques Barzun (463), R. P. Blackmur (466), Donald Davidson (576), Bonamy Dobrée (548), F. R. Leavis (499), Arthur Mizener (355), Katherine Anne Porter (521), John Crowe Ransom (526), Delmore Schwartz (529), Allen Tate (537), and Morton D. Zabel (600).
   Also contains Herbert J. Muller's 'The Novels of Hardy Today' 214–24.

107   *Studies in the Novel* 4:4 (Winter 1972)

Special Hardy number. Essays by the following authors are annotated separately: Osborne (711), Horne (702), Wing

(387), Giordano (336), Starzyk (258), Edwards (240), Martin (223), Alexander (27). Also contains Robert F. Fleissner, '"Ideas Striking, Novel, or Beautiful": A Hitherto Unpublished Comment of Hardy's' 628–9.

108   Watt, Ian (ed.)
THE VICTORIAN NOVEL: MODERN ESSAYS IN CRITICISM (London: Oxford University Press, 1971)

Reprints articles by Katherine Anne Porter (521) and Tony Tanner (316). Includes extracts from Albert J. Guerard on *MC* (131) and Irving Howe on *JO* (137).

Full-length Studies

109   Abercrombie, Lascelles
THOMAS HARDY: A CRITICAL STUDY (London:
Martin Secker, 1912)

Abercrombie values H's fiction for its tragic 'metaphysic'.
FMC, RN, MC and *W* are 'dramatic' – the lives of a variety
of characters are woven into 'a single complicated pattern of
destiny'; whereas *T* and *JO* are 'epic' – they are 'concerned
with one human theme, which goes forward in unswerving
continuity', and which enables H to add 'the gloss of his own
opinion of the tragedy'. The chapter on H's poetry (written
when only three volumes of verse had been published) shows
the perplexity of contemporary criticism in the face of his
seemingly prosaic (in Abercrombie's curious terminology,
'kinetic') style. *D,* however, is seen as a masterpiece of
'conceptual poetry', and a lengthy chapter demonstrates how
its metaphysic is projected in the form of a 'chronicle play'
within a 'drama of spirits'. This study is mainly interesting as
a kind of interim report on H's work, reflecting intelligent
contemporary critical opinion; but it is also still worth
reading for its overall view of the major novels, and
especially for its challenging estimate of *D.*

110   Bayley, John
AN ESSAY ON HARDY (Cambridge: Cambridge
University Press, 1978)

A brilliant, though also slightly tiresome, book in which
Bayley examines the texture of H's writing with ingenuity
and sensitivity, but makes some quirky and unconvincing
judgements about the relative value of the earlier and later
novels. Bayley finds positive virtue in the curiously uninte-
grated nature of H's style, resulting in a 'characteristic
instability' in which there is a sharp contrast 'between the
physical perceptions, which are always his own, and the
opinions and ideas which seldom are . . .'. At its best this
style 'has at one moment no eye for itself, as it seems, while
at the next it is assiduously concocting effects'. For Bayley H
is at his best in the poetry, in *FMC* and in odd corners of

novels like *PBE* and *TT*. In *T* the novelist who usually 'seems to keep something back' writes 'with positive abandonment', and in *JO* he betrays a coarseness of texture, which shows 'how little intensity suits H's process'.

111   Beach, Joseph Warren
THE TECHNIQUE OF THOMAS HARDY (Chicago: Chicago University Press, 1922; reprinted New York: Russell & Russell, 1962)

For Beach H's greatest artistic achievements are *RN, T* and *JO,* in each of which he subdues his liking for melodramatic contrivances of plot to a simpler structural principle. *RN* excels in the dramatic organisation of a theme, with Aristotelian unity; *T* has a simpler, popular structure geared to pathos; and *JO* is controlled by a 'drab and biting realism'. The chapter on *MC* is disappointingly imperceptive; but that on *FMC,* although it celebrates H's use of his pastoral setting rather than his narrative art, is the most interesting.
[Extracts from the chapter on *FMC* are reprinted in R. P. Draper (ed.), THOMAS HARDY: THREE PASTORAL NOVELS (91) 64–82.]

112   Berle, Lina Wright
GEORGE ELIOT AND THOMAS HARDY (New York: Mitchell Kennedy, 1917)

Berle compares H unfavourably with George Eliot: his realism is one-sided, 'he lacks scientific detachment, and he over-glorifies the liberty of the individual'. He does, however, possess 'the gift of lyric expression to a high degree'.

113   Blunden, Edmund
THOMAS HARDY (London: Macmillan, 1954)

The first two-thirds is an account of H's life and writing career, much of which has been superseded by later biographies, though the frequent quotations from contemporary reviews still have their value. The remaining one-third discusses H's fiction, *D* and the poems, and is salutary in the judicious and equal attention it gives to each. The chapter on the poems remains a sensitive and thoughtful essay in its own right. Blunden knew H in the latter years of his life, and this personal knowledge colours the portrait he paints.

114 Boumelha, Penny
THOMAS HARDY AND WOMEN: SEXUAL
IDEOLOGY AND NARRATIVE FORM (Brighton,
Sussex: Harvester Press, 1982)

After a preliminary chapter on 'sexual ideology and the "nature" of woman 1880–1900' this feminist study focuses on women and marriage in *RN, W, T* and *JO*. There is also a chapter relating H to 'women and the new fiction 1880–1900'.

115 Brennecke, Ernest, Jr
THOMAS HARDY'S UNIVERSE: A STUDY OF A
POET'S MIND (London: T. Fisher Unwin, 1924)

Although in conversation with Brennecke H disavowed 'the professional philosopher's attitude', and he seems to espouse no system, the influence of Schopenhauer's idealism (man has no objective knowledge of the world, which is 'present in his mind only as a phenomenon of consciousness') and the concept of 'the Will' are pervasive. The five attributes of the Will are all reflected in H's work: (1) it is one and immanent; (2) it is groundless and autonomous (therefore necessitarian and determinist); (3) it is unconscious; (4) it is aimless (hence H's pessimism); (5) it is indestructible (therefore allowing a faint ray of hope). This is not a work of criticism, but it has continuing value as an exposition of the basis of H's thought.

116 Brooks, Jean
THOMAS HARDY: THE POETIC STRUCTURE
(London: Elek Books, 1971). Extract reprinted in Gibson
and Johnson (eds), A CASEBOOK (429) 202–16

The seeming contradictions of H's writings are resolved by their poetic structure: 'Hardy's emotionally charged poetic pattern integrates all his personal interests into a new artistic unity.' Accordingly, Chapters 1–5 form an extended essay on H's verse, embracing the overtly philosophical poems, the shorter lyrics, the movingly personal adaptations of the elegy tradition in H's poems on the death of Emma, and the dramatic and narrative poems. This sets the tone for the remaining chapters, covering the minor fiction, each of the major novels from *FMC* to *JO,* and *D.* Throughout Brooks works by means of close, sensitive 'practical criticism' of the text, and with the emphasis on H's command of an idiosyncratic mode of expression which nevertheless focuses on the immediacy and reality of passionate feeling. This is probably the best all-round introduction to the distinctive and enduring quality of H's work.

117   Brown, Douglas
THOMAS HARDY (London: Longman, 1954; revised edition, 1961)

Brown's main theme is the 'urban invasion' of a traditional rural community, seen in the context of 'the agricultural tragedy of 1870–1902'. He is apologetic with regard to H's style, but admires its strength and the ballad-like manner of narration. Among the novels fullest treatment is given to *FMC, RN, MC, W* and *T.* Only a handful of the poems make H 'a major poet', but these are feelingly analysed, including 'During Wind and Rain', which is discussed at some length. Despite radical changes in more recent criticism, this remains an attractive and sympathetic introduction to H's fiction and poetry, laying chief emphasis on his deep humanity and the intensity of his response to rural life.

The section on *T* is reprinted in R. P. Draper (ed.), HARDY: THE TRAGIC NOVELS (90) 158–64, and the section on *W* in R. P. Draper (ed.), THOMAS HARDY: THREE PASTORAL NOVELS (91) 157–70.

Pages 166–81 of the 1954 edition are reprinted in TWENTIETH-CENTURY POETRY: CRITICAL ESSAYS AND DOCUMENTS, ed. Graham Martin and P. N. Furbank (Milton Keynes: Open University Press, 1975) 269–80.

Pages 170–81 are reprinted in Gibson and Johnson (eds), A CASEBOOK (429) 160–8.

118   Bullen, J. B.
THE EXPRESSIVE EYE: FICTION AND PERCEPTION IN THE WORK OF THOMAS HARDY (London: Oxford University Press, 1986)

This is the most comprehensive and well documented of several studies devoted to the painterly emphasis in H's fiction. It is concerned with influences, e.g. Turner, Ruskin,

Impressionism, but also develops awareness of the literary equivalents of pictorial movements in H's narrative and descriptive art and in his representation of character. The earlier work is more static than the later – the emphasis shifts from 'being' to 'becoming'. The eye is 'more agile' in *FMC*, and in *RN* watchers within the novel give way to the reader as 'the principal spectator', the creation of 'a psychological landscape' and narrative expressed 'in terms of human physiognomy'. H's professional knowledge of architecture is reflected in *L* and, more successfully, in *MC*. He makes original use of the contrast between modern and primitive modes of art in *T*, and of the subdued tonal realism of Bastien-Lepage and George Clausen in *JO*.

119   Butler, Lance St John
THOMAS HARDY (Cambridge: Cambridge University Press, 1978)

An introduction to H which focuses on the major novels, but also includes a chapter on the minor fiction and one on the poems. H's major theme is love and the tension 'between the possible and the actual'. In the fiction there is a progression from the balanced treatment of individuals, rustic 'chorus' and environment in *FMC* through greater allegorical and cosmic emphasis in *RN* and *MC* to the more intensive focus on individuals in a multi-dimensional context of *T* and *JO*. *JO*, 'the first modern novel', is unprecedentedly frank in its treatment of the conflict between sex and spirit. Butler is both shrewd and sensitive in his critical analysis, while keeping the needs of the inexperienced reader of H well in mind.

120   Carpenter, Richard C.
THOMAS HARDY (New York: Twayne's English Authors Series, Twayne, 1964)

Like Guerard's 1949 study (131), this reflects the changing fortunes of H's critical reputation in the post-World War II period, with a downgrading of his 'philosophy' and architectonic skill accompanying stronger appreciation of his intuitive and imaginative powers. Carpenter particularly stresses H's use of symbol and myth to give resonance to his fiction. Each novel is given its own survey at an introductory level. Chapter 2, 'The Minor Strain', covers *DR, UGT, PBE,*

HE, TM, L, TT, WB and the short stories (including 'On the Western Circuit' and 'The Romantic Adventures of a Milkmaid'). Chapter 3, 'The Major Chord', covers *FMC, RN, MC, W, T* and *JO: MC*, centred on Henchard, is the most disciplined artistically of the novels, *W* the least coherent, *T* a masterpiece because of the elemental femininity and the folk-tale resonance of the heroine, and *JO* distils 'the final measure of his irony in fiction'. Chapter 4, on the poems and *D,* is disappointing: only some 15–20 of H's poems are major; they suffer from a naïve separation between 'form' and 'idea', the imposition of a poetically barren 'philosophy' and excessive use of irony. *D* is 'panoramic and historical rather than dramatic', lacks character development, and its chief figure, Napoleon, is oversimplified.

121   Casagrande, Peter J.
UNITY IN HARDY'S NOVELS: 'REPETITIVE
SYMMETRIES' (London: Macmillan, 1982)

Casagrande emphasises the recurrence of two main themes throughout H's fiction and much of his poetry – 'return' to one's native place or an early ideal, and attempted 'restoration' of what has gone wrong. Both are seen as blighted by an inherent life-process of 'irremediable decay', which, however, can also be the source of a new kind of bleak beauty. Biographical connections are made with H's own return to Dorset, his loss of faith, his disenchantment with love and his disillusionment with his architect's work of restoration. The theme of return is exemplified in *UGT, RN, W* and the Emma poems; restoration in *FMC, MC, T* and *JO* – the last two being considered together as a 'diptych' echoing, and contrasting with, each other. Evidence is sometimes forced for the sake of 'repetitive symmetries' and a perhaps too Mahler-like portrait of H emerges, but this is an interesting, and well-written, attempt to establish a coherently unified pattern in H's life and work.

The section on *UGT* is reprinted in R. P. Draper (ed.), THOMAS HARDY: THREE PASTORAL NOVELS (91) 111–15.

122   Cecil, Lord David
HARDY THE NOVELIST: AN ESSAY IN CRITICISM
(London: Constable, 1943)

This is a lucidly written essay, rather than critical study, on H's strengths and weaknesses. Cecil includes the pictorial and poetic quality of H's imagination, the broadly human appeal of his characters and his emotional intensity among the strengths, and the lack of 'design', the want of restraint and H's isolation from the mainstream of culture in his time among the weaknesses. H's affinities were with Shakespeare, Fielding and Scott rather than with Austen, Eliot and James: he was 'a man born after his time . . . the last representative of the tradition and spirit of the Elizabethan drama', but without the faith of the Elizabethans. A number of Cecil's comments seem superficial in the light of more recent criticism, and some of his judgements ill-considered, but the book remains a highly readable introduction to H's fiction.

123   Chew, Samuel C.
THOMAS HARDY: POET AND NOVELIST (Bryn Mawr College, New York: Longmans, Green and Co., 1921)

Four major novels: *RN, MC, T, JO*. With *MC* H changes to concentration on one figure rather than several. *MC* is 'H's most artistic achievement'. Abandons objectivity in *T:* 'he has a thesis to propound and he does so in a recriminating fashion'. Less objective still in *JO*, but excels in 'the promulgation of new and important ideas'.

124   Dave, Jagdish Chandra
THE HUMAN PREDICAMENT IN HARDY'S NOVELS (London: Macmillan, 1985)

This is not so much a work of scholarship or literary criticism as an attempt to define H's philosophical position from an oriental point of view. H is compared with thinkers like Schopenhauer, Sartre and Camus who find the human predicament 'absurd', but he is not seen as existentialist. He has greater affinity with Pythagoras and Marcus Aurelius 'in holding philosophy . . . as an ethical response to the world inspired by the longing to get beyond the suffering of the human condition'. But above all he resembles Buddha in regarding the true goal as the achievement of a state of beneficent detachment. The conclusion is of doubtful value, but some useful points are established on the way.

125   Duffin, H.C.
        THOMAS HARDY (Manchester: Manchester University
        Press, 1916; revised editions, 1921, 1937)

        An overlengthy and somewhat gushingly overwritten study,
        covering the entire span of H's work. The novels are
        summarised, and chapters are devoted to aspects of H's
        fictional technique and his philosophy. Though it is as a
        novelist that Duffin rates H highest, his sections on *D* and
        the poems remain the most useful. He gives a clear account
        of *D*, singling out the stage directions for special attention;
        and though he relegates H to secondary rank among poets,
        he is full and interesting in his treatment of the poems.

126   Elliott, Albert Pettigrew
        FATALISM IN THE WORKS OF THOMAS HARDY
        (New York: Russell & Russell, 1935; reprinted 1966)

        Although Elliott rejects the notion that H's work is informed
        by a consistent philosophy, he maintains that there is an
        innate melancholy suffusing the poetry and the fiction which
        issues in a pervasive 'fataiism'. In earlier works this takes the
        form of incidental chance happenings, but in later works
        there is a more organised sense of determinism. Separate
        chapters are devoted to five manifestations of Fate: chance
        and coincidence; time; nature; women; convention and law.
        Unfortunately Elliott falls foul of the very systematising
        tendency which he recognises as inappropriate to criticism of
        H's work. Later commentators have exposed the flaws in this
        approach, but there remain some useful insights in this
        wide-ranging, but compact survey.

127   Enstice, Andrew
        THOMAS HARDY: LANDSCAPES OF THE MIND
        (London: Macmillan, 1979)

        Fascinating exploration of H's Wessex and its history. Enstice
        makes it clear that H did not try to give exact descriptions of
        the area, and arbitrarily altered his landscapes when he
        wanted. 'The general nature of each area was the basis for its
        selection by Hardy; he has merely selected the necessary
        material to emphasise that nature, and excluded extraneous
        detail.' Begins with chapter on *MC*, since this is the novel
        most obviously based on an actual place. Proceeds to

examine *UGT* and its successors, all of which are about small remote communities. In *T* and *JO,* the focus is on an individual who moves about a good deal; the community is less important and many towns are mere place names.

Part of the chapter on *FMC* is reprinted in R. P. Draper (ed.), THOMAS HARDY: THREE PASTORAL NOVELS (91) 146–56.

128 Giordano, Frank R.
'I'D HAVE MY LIFE UNBE': THOMAS HARDY'S SELF-DESTRUCTIVE CHARACTERS (Alabama: University of Alabama Press, 1984)

Giordano concentrates on the suicidal impulse in many of H's heroes and heroines. Special attention is paid to Eustacia (*RN*) and Henchard (*MC*), who are seen as 'egoistic suicides' (Giordano recognises the ambiguity surrounding Eustacia's death, but supports the suicide hypothesis); to Jude, who, along with Boldwood (*FMC*), is seen as an 'anomic suicide'; and to Giles and Tess, 'altruistic suicides'. Self-destructiveness is the logical outcome of 'the modernist premises', and H is praised for facing these honestly – suicide cannot be dismissed as mere madness. On the other hand, 'through the self-destruction of his characters, he asserts life's fragile preciousness most dramatically', and so heightens the sense of the need for love.

129 Gregor, Ian
THE GREAT WEB: THE FORM OF HARDY'S MAJOR FICTION (London: Faber & Faber, 1974)

Gregor's concern is to explore the nature of H's fiction as 'unfolding process' and to insist on the inseparability of character and ideas. He confines himself to the 'major fiction', with separate chapters devoted to *FMC, RN, MC, W, T* and *JO,* and operates by means of close analysis of episodes and passages which illustrate the interaction of the fictional elements, including the voice of the narrator. The result is an intelligent and sensitive, though also elusive and sometimes unnecessarily difficult, examination of the novels as something like poetic texts, but with full value given to story rather than image and symbol. The best chapters are the last two: that on *T* interestingly argues for a change in the heroine from subjective consciousness to more emphatic recognition of the outside forces which work upon her; and that on *JO* shows how Sue and Jude's attempt to live the 'free' life inevitably succumbs to the pressures of society. *JO* in particular is seen as verging on a more modern kind of fiction which points the way that D. H. Lawrence was to follow.

[Extracts from the chapter on *JO* are reprinted in R. P. Draper (ed.), HARDY: THE TRAGIC NOVELS (90) 227–47.]

130   Grundy, Joan
HARDY AND THE SISTER ARTS (London and Basingstoke: Macmillan, 1979)

In this examination of H's debt to the non-literary arts Grundy emphasises the emotive effect of allusions to, and methods adapted from, painting, sculpture, the theatre, music and dance; and in a chapter on the 'cinematic arts' she also demonstrates his anticipation, especially in *D,* of the more 'dynamic, fluid, powerfully visual art' of the modern cinema and television. Like other nineteenth-century artists H has a highly developed aesthetic sense (though in his case firmly grounded in popular art-forms such as melodrama and folk-song) which moves him towards an interweaving of all the arts into one evocative whole. His affinity to the blended musico-dramatic form of opera is given some particularly interesting pages, as are his 'Impressionist' effects in *T.* This is an important study of H's sensibility and technique, worked out with much illuminatingly close detail.

131   Guerard, Albert J.
THOMAS HARDY: THE NOVELS AND STORIES (London: Oxford University Press; Cambridge, Mass.: Harvard University Press, 1949; reprinted 1964). Extracts in Albert J. Guerard (ed.) (93) 63–70, and in Ian Watt (ed.) (108) 401–6

A pioneering study in its emphasis on H as an 'anti-realist' rather than a realist and as a teller of tales rather than a philosopher or craftsman. Much of Guerard's critical effort is directed to showing H's inadequacies, but he also has interesting things to say about H's women, especially their development from fickleness and coquetry to more deeply understood characters, and the 'unaggressive tendency' so conspicuous in his men. H's one great tragic hero is Henchard. Guerard's conclusion is that H is 'a great popular novelist and not a great deliberate artist'. A well-written study which moves thematically rather than chronologically, with the consequence that comments on individual novels and stories tend to be scattered. The 1964 reprint includes a chapter on H's poetry.

132   Halliday, F. E.
THOMAS HARDY: HIS LIFE AND WORK (Bath:
Adams & Dart, 1972)

Written in the form of a biography, with accounts of the published works and their critical reception interpolated at appropriate points, this is an easily read, but superficial, introductory guide rather than a critical study. Some well-chosen illustrations are also included.

133   Hasan, Noorul
THOMAS HARDY: THE SOCIOLOGICAL
IMAGINATION (London: Macmillan, 1982)

Hasan argues that H's Wessex was a product of 'sociological imagination', based on historical facts, but giving 'an imaginative response to those facts'. In detailed analyses of *FMC, RN, MC, W, T, JO* and the shorter fiction, the constant standard of appraisal is a realistic, rather than romantic or pastoralised, appreciation of rural culture and community – though *JO* is 'an expression of Hardy's dismay and bewilderment at the final disruption of the rural community'. Hasan frequently refers to previous critics, but presents his own, often dissenting, views in a clear and reasonable manner.

134   Hawkins, Desmond
THOMAS HARDY (London: Arthur Barker, 1950)

Devoted to the novels only, this brief, attractively written essay is a little 'belle-lettrist' in manner, but pointed and refreshingly independent. H is seen as weak in characterisation and narrative structure, but strong in 'vivid and sensitive delineation of the Wessex scene' and in poetic power. He is also a practitioner of 'the sex-novel' in a way that makes it epitomise man's destiny.

135   Hedgcock, F. A.
THOMAS HARDY: PENSEUR ET ARTISTE (Paris:
Librairie Hachette, 1911)

Although H disliked some of the biographical comments
made in the opening pages of this French study, the author's
main purpose was to correct two fallacies of contemporary
criticism: (1) that H was a 'naturalist' of the Zola school, and
(2) that he was a mere story-teller. Hedgcock argues that
there is a consistent, if pessimistic, philosophy running
through H's work, and that he is to be seen as an imaginative
and emotional rather than realistic writer. However, his
artistic achievement is at its best in *RN*. In *T* and *JO* there is
evidence that his work has in fact been adversely affected by
the scientific doctrines of the naturalists.

136   Hornback, Bert G.
THE METAPHOR OF CHANCE: VISION AND
TECHNIQUE IN THE WORKS OF THOMAS HARDY
(Athens, Ohio: Ohio University Press, 1971)

H has twin perceptions with regard to man and his world:
man is determined by it, but also a free being, the victim of
coincidence, but able to learn to accept his situation and
make it his own. This is reflected in H's treatment of the
Wessex environment. For example, in *RN* the setting
embodies the immensities of time and space dominating man;
Eustacia fails to respond to this challenge, Clym – the true
hero of the novel – identifies himself with the heath. There
are also chapters on the minor novels, *MC, T, JO,* the poetry
and *D*.

137   Howe, Irving
THOMAS HARDY (New York: Macmillan; London:
Collier-Macmillan, 1976). Extract in Ian Watt (ed.) (108)
432–45

Howe alternates between broad impressions of H's work and
more precise analysis. He sees H as neither wholly traditional
nor modernist, but 'sustaining friction one with the other',
and as 'a writer struggling towards expressionist and sym-
bolist fiction at a time when the only tradition immediately
available to him was the conventional realism of the

nineteenth century'. Chief emphasis among the novels is given to *MC, T* and *JO*. The chapter on *D* is largely concerned with its impossibility as an epic; that on the lyrics is more sympathetic than its repetition of the standard judgement that the number of good poems is small would suggest. Some critics maintain that this is the best general introduction to H. It is certainly among the best: elegantly written, laced with an attractive sense of humour and warmly responsive to H's personality, but also slightly condescending at times and a little too preoccupied with the need 'to grade properly'.

138   Hyman, Virginia R.
ETHICAL PERSPECTIVE IN THE NOVELS OF
THOMAS HARDY (Port Washington, New York:
Kennikat Press, 1975)

Hyman argues that H saw character as varying with social development and that he accepted the Comtean view of ethical evolution from egotism to altruism. His characters are judged according to their ability to transcend egotism: thus Eustacia is seen as a type of 'the romantic egotist', but Clym evolves. There are studies also of 'the evolution of Tess' and 'the disillusionment of Jude'. Hyman makes some useful points, but does not sufficiently differentiate H's ethical position from that of George Eliot.

139   Jekel, Pamela L.
THOMAS HARDY'S HEROINES: A CHORUS OF
PRIORITIES (New York: Whitston Publishing Company,
1986)

H deals with the Victorian stereotype woman, but also succeeds in giving 'a portrait of the whole woman trapped within such an image'. Jekel attempts a comprehensive commentary on all H's main female characters. The most useful chapters are those on *HE* ('the tale of an artist, a unique and individual woman who must give up love . . . for power and a sort of freedom'), *JO* and *WB*. Somewhat ineptly written, and an uneven mixture of the derivative and the occasionally original, this is a contribution to feminist criticism of H which at least credits him with sympathetic insight into the social and psychological problems of women.

140   Johnson, Bruce
TRUE CORRESPONDENCE: A PHENOMENOLOGY
OF THOMAS HARDY'S NOVELS (Tallahassee, Florida:
Florida State University Press, 1983)

Johnson argues that H's imagination has a fundamentally
phenomenological bent which emphasises 'the significance of
the nonhuman in the human'. The pastoral concept of 'otium'
and the sense of continuity between man and nature are
embodied in characters like Oak, Winterborne and Tess, and
opposed to them are characters like Troy, Angel Clare and
Sue who embody an inimical form of intellectual isolation.
FMC shows Bathsheba caught between these opposing
forces, but finally achieving a maturity which combines her
independent spirit with the 'survival' qualities of Oak; in *RN*
Egdon Heath represents the phenomenological continuity
rather than tragedy; *T* implies that the ideal state of
consciousness, which includes knowledge of one's deepest
primal energies, exists in Tess herself, but that it is frustrated
by the imposition of false Christian ideals; and *JO* represents
this 'survival' consciousness in a tragically decayed condition.
Unfortunately, the underlying philosophical theme is not
explicitly stated, with the result that this is a difficult book for
readers unfamiliar with the ideas of Husserl. It is, however,
an original and intermittently illuminating study which
affords important new insights into H's novels.

141   Johnson, Lionel
THE ART OF THOMAS HARDY (London: Mathews &
Lane, 1894; revised edition, 1922)

This first book-length study of H's work is concerned with
the novels only. It is still valuable for its shrewd analysis of
the general characteristics of H's fiction. The 2nd edition
includes a chapter on the poetry added by J. E. Barton.
   [Brief extract in R. P. Draper (ed.), HARDY: THE
TRAGIC NOVELS (90) 55–7.]

142   Johnson, Trevor
THOMAS HARDY (London: Evans Brothers Ltd, 1968)

This brief introduction to H, in the 'Literature in Perspective'
series, is unusual in giving pride of place to the poems rather
than the novels – though the latter also receive adequate

attention. Discussion is broken up by an excess of sub-headings and themes, but Johnson's enthusiasm for his subject comes through strongly, making this a particularly useful book for younger readers.

143   Kramer, Dale
THOMAS HARDY: THE FORMS OF TRAGEDY
(Detroit, Michigan: Wayne State University Press; London: Macmillan, 1975)

Kramer's emphasis is on the variable relation of structure and tragic vision in H's novels. Each of the major novels has its own 'dominant aesthetic feature' creating 'the peculiar quality of tragedy that distinguishes it'. *FMC* relies uneasily on a series of schematic oppositions. *RN* juxtaposes the values of Eustacia and Clym and places them in paradoxical relation to Egdon Heath. In a more firmly controlled tragic pattern Henchard and Farfrae in *MC* are made representatives of a cycle of rise and fall. In *W* there is a lack of focus on one tragically distinguished protagonist, and instead the tragic feeling is diffused throughout a group who suffer the frustrations which are imposed on them by society and reflected in their natural environment. In *T* and *JO* the tragic form is based in consciousness and perception: 'the subjective creation of significance in a sensitive and serious consciousness' is at the centre of the tragic experience in *T;* and in *JO* a peculiarly Hardyan 'point of view' method (contrary to the accepted opinion that this is the most didactic of his novels) makes for a 'pervasive relativism'. This is a thoughtful and exacting study, and, though questionable in some of its conclusions, one that demands careful consideration.

144   Lawrence, D. H.
STUDY OF THOMAS HARDY (in PHOENIX: THE POSTHUMOUS PAPERS OF D. H. LAWRENCE, ed. Edward D. McDonald (London: Heinemann, 1936))

Written in 1914–15, though not published till 1936 (six years after Lawrence's death), this has become one of the most celebrated, and most frequently quoted, of all studies of H. Much of it is an exposition of Lawrence's ideas on the purpose of life and the relations between the sexes, but within this context he also makes penetratingly original comments on H's novels. H's heroes and heroines 'are struggling hard to come into being' and 'always shooting suddenly out of a tight convention'. But their tragedies lack the inevitability which results from conflict with fundamental forces of nature: of Eustacia, Tess, Sue and Jude Lawrence says that 'the judgment of men killed them, not the judgment of their own souls or the judgment of Eternal God'. His interpretation of *T* anticipates later emphasis on the destructive intellectualism of Angel Clare, and is surprisingly favourable to Alec Durberville. In his comments on *JO* he is also unusually sympathetic to Arabella, while Sue is presented as a specialised type of modern woman, overdeveloped spiritually and null in the body. His view of *RN* stresses the permanence and 'instinctive life' of Egdon Heath.

145   Macdonell, Annie
        THOMAS HARDY (New York: Dodd, Mead & Co., 1985; reprinted Folcroft Library Editions, 1922)

Interesting chiefly as an early study of H, written before the publication of *JO*. Macdonell surveys the novels up to *WB* and adds chapters of a rather superficial kind on his craftsmanship, characterisation, humour, style, painting of nature and 'Wessex' (the latter mostly geographical). H's unconventionality is a recurrent theme.

146   Meisel, Perry
        THOMAS HARDY: THE RETURN OF THE REPRESSED (New Haven and London: Yale University Press, 1972)

An interesting, if slightly obscure and pretentious, study of 'the major fiction', with chapters on 'the early novels' (*UGT*, *PBE* and *FMC*), *RN, MC, W, T* and *JO*. Beginning with the conflicting tendencies in H's mind as a result of his being both a member of the traditional Wessex community and a detached, conceptualising nineteenth-century rationalist, Meisel attempts to show how the predilections fostered by such a divided condition increasingly influence the structures, characters and 'poetics' of H's novels. *MC* marks the crucial stage in this process, but its fulfilment is seen in the individualising self-consciousness attributed to Tess and Jude. Darwin and Freud provide the intellectual reference points marking this route, and its terminus is the psychological awareness enshrined in the distinctly 'modern' novel of Joyce and Lawrence.

147 Miller, J. Hillis
THOMAS HARDY: DISTANCE AND DESIRE
(Cambridge, Mass.: Harvard University Press, 1970)

Miller 'tries to identify in the mass of H's writings the hidden structure which will allow a comprehensive view of them all'. The dualistic components of the pattern which results are 'distance', a detached viewer's stance with regard to the world, and 'desire', signifying involvement, especially via sexual love, and consequent loss of self-possession. H's art transcends this dualism by providing a means of indirect response – participating yet holding at a distance. In the fiction H's narrator exemplifies 'a paradoxical combination of proximity and distance, presence and absence, sympathy and coldness'. In the poetry illusion and disillusion reflect a similar opposition; and in *D* the immediate ignorance of the personae contrasts with a remoter conscious perspective in which they are seen as creatures of the Immanent Will. Illumination, which comes to H's characters through suffering, causes them to wish for annihilation, but H's art both perpetuates and redeems the past. Probably the most ambitious structuralist interpretation of H's work, this is also the most eloquent and the most modest: Miller acknowledges the subjectivity and distortion entailed in all such readings. However, he avoids the merely arbitrary, and manages to combine generalisation with effective illustration and analysis. The different areas of H's work are drawn on throughout Miller's study, and it is difficult therefore to specify treatment of particular works. There are interesting comments on all the major novels and many of the minor, especially *WB*. Attention is focused on theme and point of view in *D,* and H's poems on the death of Emma receive some extended treatment. At various points there are illuminating comparisons with Proust.

148 Millgate, Michael
THOMAS HARDY: HIS CAREER AS A NOVELIST
(London: The Bodley Head, 1971). Extract on *UGT* is
reprinted in R. P. Draper (ed.), THOMAS HARDY:
THREE PASTORAL NOVELS (91) 97–106

Written in an admirably clear, unpretentious style, this is one of the most permanently useful studies of H's novels. Each one is given full and judicious independent treatment, but set in its context in H's developing career as a writer, with appropriate reference to his biography, his views and revisions, and the comments of reviewers and H's reactions to these. *DR, UGT* and *PBE* are treated as part of H's 'Apprenticeship' (though the excellent essay on *UGT* shows it to be, within limits, an early masterpiece); *FMC, HE* and *RN* represent his first phase of 'Achievement'; there is 'Recession' with *TM, L* and *TT,* 'Renewal' with *MC* and *W,* and 'Fulfilment' with *T, WB* and *JO.* Millgate also gives careful consideration to H's conception and realisation of the idea of 'Wessex', and in his final chapter makes an illuminating comparison between H and Faulkner as regional novelists and modern adaptors of the pastoral. H and Henry James are also compared.

149   Morrell, Roy
       THOMAS HARDY: THE WILL AND THE WAY
       (Singapore: University of Malaya Press, 1965). Extract on
       FMC is reprinted in R. P. Draper (ed.), THOMAS
       HARDY: THREE PASTORAL NOVELS (91) 116–28

The allusion in the title to the saying 'Where there's a will there's a way' indicates the burden of this study: it is an attempt to refute the established view that H is pessimistic and fatalistic. Properly understood his novels, and also *D,* show his belief in man's capacity to choose and to exert himself effectively against adverse circumstances; when he fails to do so it is by his own fault. Gabriel Oak in *FMC* is the representative example of one who resists wisely. The thesis is well argued, but over-polemical, and leads in the end to underestimation of the tragic force in H's writing.

150   Nevinson, Henry W.
       THOMAS HARDY (London: Allen & Unwin, 1941)

Partly devoted to personal reminiscences of H and his sayings. Notable in giving such prominence to the poetry and *D.*

151   Orel, Harold
       THE UNKNOWN THOMAS HARDY: LESSER KNOWN

ASPECTS OF HARDY'S LIFE AND CAREER (Brighton, Sussex: Harvester Press, 1987)

Seven chapters discuss H's interest in the theatre, the law, architecture and archaeology, and Orel also describes his literary friendships.

152   Page, Norman
THOMAS HARDY (London: Routledge & Kegan Paul, 1977)

A sensible, clear, unpretentiously written survey of the whole of H's literary career, embracing novels, short stories, poems, *D*, the *Life* (which Page calls 'Hardy's Autobiography'), the non-fictional prose and the notebooks and diaries. Page is particularly good on the 'pictorialism' of H's narrative technique: 'It may not be too wild an exaggeration to suggest that to read a typical Hardy novel is like visiting the Royal Academy in the mid-Victorian period'. The major novels are discussed collectively, but the minor novels individually. It is thus easy to find succinct self-contained pieces on *DR*, *PBE*, *HE*, *TM*, *L*, *TT* and *WB;* but there are excellent comments, e.g. on *W*, *T* and *JO*, included in the thematic treatment of the major novels. A full and interesting chapter is devoted to the 'Verse', which is particularly good on H's diction. As a general introduction to H's work and the critical issues which it raises this is one of the best available books.

153   Pinion, Frank B.
THOMAS HARDY: ART AND THOUGHT (London: Macmillan, 1977)

A series of discrete essays on facets of H's work. Subjects include the influence of Wilkie Collins, Shelley and Richardson; the elements of chance and choice in H's treatment of the fates of his characters; H's humour; the use of myth in *RN*, *W*, *T* and *JO;* the question of Tess's purity; H's tendency to idealise women; and his substitution of a positivist life-after-death in the form of memory for the Christian idea of immortality. The most interesting essay is on H's 'Pictorial Art', which deals with his frequent allusion to painters, and classifies his own descriptions under three categories: (a) those which are 'basic and direct', (b) those 'where more is meant than meets the eye', and (c) those which are psychological – 'a concrete and sometimes poetic way of expressing states of mind, feelings, and moods in the protagonists themselves'. The quality of the essays varies considerably, but they are the work of a scholar who is exceptionally well informed about H and able to draw on a wealth of examples.

154   Salter, Charles H.
GOOD LITTLE THOMAS HARDY (London: Macmillan, 1981)

Salter's is 'a largely negative and destructive approach', intended, however, to 'restore to the reader his freedom to respond to Hardy in what, to Hardy, can be the only right way – simply'. Many excesses of H scholarship and criticism are pugnaciously dealt with, but Salter has comparatively little to offer in the way of positive insights of his own. The book is worth mentioning, however, for its brisk, no-nonsense attitude which at least clears the ground of some accumulated intellectual rubbish.

155   Scott-James, R. A.
THOMAS HARDY (London: British Council, Writers and Their Work series, Longmans, 1951)

This sketch concentrates on the novels and *D;* the poems are scarcely mentioned. It remains useful for those who wish to take a brief, preliminary look at H's life and work.

156   Sherman, G. W.
THE PESSIMISM OF THOMAS HARDY (Rutherford, Madison, Teaneck: Fairleigh Dickinson University Press, 1976)

Sherman's interpretation of H presents him as a frustrated radical and his 'pessimism' as 'the result of his disillusionment with the promise of his age after 1867'. The fiction is divided into 'Wessex' and 'London' novels (*PBE* and *JO* rather surprisingly being included among the latter). Emphasis is given to H's sympathy for the working class, the corollary of which is hostility to the upper classes, and, especially in *D,* his anti-war sentiments. As criticism this repetitious and excessively lengthy (518pp) Marxist study is of very limited

value; but it usefully reminds us of H's context in nineteenth-
and twentieth-century political, social and economic history,
and, biased though it is, draws attention to a neglected
dimension of H's work.

157   Southerington, F. R.
     HARDY'S VISION OF MAN (London: Chatto & Windus,
     1971)

This is a study of H's philosophy and also of his personal
temperament, with the latter taking precedence, since Southerington holds that H's 'eventual beliefs owed more to his
frame of mind than his frame of mind owed to his beliefs'.
Both, however, are given full measure. The novels are seen
as falling into two broad categories, 'personal' (e.g. *UGT*,
PBE and *JO*) and 'ideological' (e.g. *FMC*, *RN* and *MC*) –
though there is no suggestion that the latter are novels of
ideas. A long section is devoted to *D* and its dual nature as
'historical drama' and 'philosophical poem'. There is a
central, but fruitful paradox in *D* in that the Will is
represented as unconscious, yet the sum of conscious beings.
This contradiction is resolved by the emergence of a tentative
conception of consciousness as gradually informing the Will
itself. Southerington gives undue emphasis to Lois Deacon's
speculations on H's affair with Tryphena Sparks, but in
general he maintains a reasonable balance between biographical and intellectual material. Incidental commentary on
the novels is thoughtful, and the analysis of the intellectual
structure of *D* is indispensable reading for students of that
work.

158   Springer, Marlene
     HARDY'S USE OF ALLUSION (London and
     Basingstoke: Macmillan, 1983)

Springer argues that H's allusiveness has been underesti-
mated as part of the ponderous self-consciousness of the
so-called 'audodidact'. He manipulates quotation and reference to give his fiction depth, complexity and irony. From
stumbling attempts in *DR* and *UGT* he progresses through
greater refinement in *PBE* and *FMC* to 'stylistic maturity' in
RN, *T* and *JO*. This study makes a useful contribution to

serious interpretation of H's work and is particularly interesting on the theme of the Arnoldian dualism between the 'Hellenistic' and the 'Hebraic'.

159   Stewart, J. I. M.
THOMAS HARDY: A CRITICAL BIOGRAPHY
(London: Longman, 1971)

Initial chapters discuss the *Life,* three women in H's life (Tryphena, Emma and Florence Henniker), his temperamental pessimism and the theme of 'urban invasion' (in Douglas Brown's phrase), about which Stewart is sceptical. All the fiction is surveyed (with footnoted summaries of plots): more than usually sympathetic attention is paid to *DR* and *PBE; MC* is judged to be not so much classical as Byronically 'romantic tragedy'; *T* is 'one of the greatest distillations of emotion into art'; and *JO* is 'fatigued and awkward' in its treatment of its hero, but Sue Bridehead makes it 'among the most impressively exploratory and intuitive of modern English novels'. The short stories and *HE, TM, L, TT* and *WB* are clumped together as 'Minor fiction'. The chapters on *D* and H's 'Major poetry' are disappointing: H is dubbed 'an obsessional poet', the good poems mingling with a much larger number of indifferent ones. Stewart writes in a clear, witty style and is rarely boring. In a level-headed and determinedly sensible manner he presents H as 'an uneven writer' whose melodramatic technique and mortuary preoccupations are offset by 'a poetic and symbolic imagination'.

160   Sumner, Rosemary
THOMAS HARDY: PSYCHOLOGICAL NOVELIST
(London: Macmillan, 1981)

Argues that H is a pioneer novelist anticipating many of the discoveries of modern psychologists such as Freud, Jung and Adler with regard to neuroses, but that he is interested in the complexity and variety of human nature rather than clinical analysis as such. Hints of lesbianism and bisexuality are traced in *DR* and *L; WB* is interpreted in terms of Jung's 'concept of the anima' and Boldwood (*FMC*) is seen as an early example of a character suffering from repressed sexuality. The chapter on *MC* concentrates on Henchard and the psychology of aggression, with its close relationship to self-destruction. Three chapters on 'psychological problems of modern man and woman' are concerned with the characters of Eustacia and Clym (*RN*), Knight (*PBE*), Angel (*T*) and Jude and Sue (*JO*). 'In *Tess,* Hardy raises the problem of society's disapproval of "the flesh" and pleads for a change'. In *JO,* 'the central contrast is between well-balanced, resilient Jude and neurotic, vulnerable Sue'. This book makes a valuable contribution to the study of H's methods of characterisation and produces some interesting revaluations (e.g. Jude). Despite its frequent references to psychiatric theory it is not over-technical, and is easily accessible to the general reader. The primary emphasis is literary critical, and the conclusions strongly underline the breadth of H's intellectual and emotional sympathies.

161   Symons, Arthur
A STUDY OF THOMAS HARDY (London: Chas. J. Sawyer, Ltd, 1927)

A slight, whimsical, but occasionally penetrating sketch (rather than 'study') of H's manner as novelist and poet. Symons is particularly impressed by H's treatment of women, and traces some surprising affinities between him and the French novelists.

162   Thurley, Geoffrey
THE PSYCHOLOGY OF HARDY'S NOVELS: THE NERVOUS AND THE STATUESQUE (St Lucia, Queensland, Australia: University of Queensland Press, 1975)

H is grouped with those writers who show a 'typological bent' in their characterisation. His major concern is with 'the laws of human relationship', with 'type-polarities and the magnetic fields of attraction', and it is from the fundamental conflicts which these generate that his tragic effects derive.

163   Vigar, Penelope
THE NOVELS OF THOMAS HARDY: ILLUSION AND REALITY (London: Athlone Press, 1974)

'Hardy's pervasive theme in all his novels – the contrast between appearance and reality – is also, consistently, the most important factor in their artistic construction.' Vigar dwells on the 'narrative pictures' which recur in H's work and the visual impressionism which builds his characters, their world and the values by which they live. *DR* and *L* illustrate his 'experiments and mistakes' with this artistic method. *UGT* and *TM* are seen as successful, but slight performances. The masterpieces are *FMC, RN, MC* and *T* – the most intensely poetic and mystically dreamy of his novels. *JO* is uneasily characterised as powerful, but ill-balanced. The theme is vigorously pursued throughout the book, and supported by effective analysis. However, it offers a strong, and significant, point of view rather than an all-round consideration of the novels.

164   Webster, Harvey Curtis
ON A DARKLING PLAIN: THE ART AND THOUGHT
OF THOMAS HARDY (Chicago and Cambridge:
University of Chicago Press, 1947)

This study of the development of H's philosophy and its embodiment in his work (chiefly the novels) extends from *DR* to *D*. H's so-called pessimism is related to the disillusioning change from his early years as a 'churchy', believing youth to his adult contact with nineteenth-century scientific rationalism, particularly in Darwin and the contributors to *Essays and Reviews.* Up to *RN* he was mainly a determinist, but the growth of sociological ideas and concomitant reform movements towards the end of the century led him to give greater emphasis (in *W* and *T,* for example) to social ills which were at least capable of remedy. *JO* became both the most pessimistic and the most meliorist of his novels. In his later work H also moved towards the view that consciousness might ultimately 'inform the Will' to the extent of overcoming mere determinism. *D* was the fruit of this development: 'the consummation of more than fifty years of honest and intelligent thought about the nature of the universal by a great thinker and poet'.

165   White, R. J.
THOMAS HARDY AND HISTORY (London: Macmillan, 1974) [edited and completed by James Gibson]

Though not a professional historian, H was fascinated by historical material, especially eye-witness accounts and aural reminiscences of Dorset in the period after the French Revolution. *TM* is H's 'solitary piece of historical reconstruction in the proper use of that term'. Five chapters are devoted to *D:* 'The historians', 'Hardy and Napoleon', 'The anti-heroes', 'Collectives, crowds, caterpillars' and 'Hardy and Tolstoy'. An interesting commentary on H's temperament rather than a critical study.

166 Williams, Merryn
A PREFACE TO HARDY (London and New York: Longman, 1976)

A useful students' introduction to H's work and its background. Part 1 deals with H's life, his rural connections (including 'William Barnes and "provincialism"') and his context in the artistic and intellectual history of Victorian England. Part 2 is a brief critical survey, including comments on six of H's heroes, an interpretative study of *MC* and commentary on ten of H's poems. Part 3 includes short biographies of figures connected with H or influential in his work, a gazetteer of places and suggestions for further reading. Illustrations accompany the text.

167 Williams, Merryn
THOMAS HARDY AND RURAL ENGLAND (London: Macmillan, 1972)

Part 1 surveys agricultural history 1840–1900 and sketches the tradition of country writing, including the work of Richard Jeffries and novelists such as Kingsley, Gaskell and George Eliot. Part 2 comments on country life and characters in H's novels, from *UGT* to *T* and *JO*. The main emphasis is on his realism and empathy with ordinary working folk, which is 'extended and complicated by questions of education, mobility, and aspiration, beyond the customary rural ways'.

168 Wing, George
HARDY, Writers and Critics Series (Edinburgh and London: Oliver and Boyd, 1963)

This is a brief, brusque introduction to H which approaches him, unusually, by way of the themes of 'betrayal and the grotesque' as exemplified in his short stories. 'The terminology of rifle shooting' is then used to score the success of the novels in terms of 'outers' (*DR, PBE, HE, L, TT* and *WB*), 'inners' (*UGT, FMC, RN, W*) and 'bulls' (*MC, T, JO*). *D* and the poetry are treated briefly in one chapter, and a final chapter, also brief, summarises critical attitudes to H.

169   Wotton, George
         THOMAS HARDY: TOWARDS A MATERIALIST
         CRITICISM (Totowa, N.J.: Barnes and Noble, 1985)

Wotton argues that the function of 'materialist criticism' is 'to produce a knowledge of writing as a social product and literature as a social relation and to bring an end to the system in which writing is used as an ideological weapon in the furtherance of social inequality'. Analysis is devoted to the ways in which H's presentation of Wessex and its people is both determined by, and implicitly critical of, nineteenth-century class-based ideology, which is itself said to be determined by economic forces. Wotton also includes some elements of a feminist critique which similarly attempts to demonstrate how H's work 'reflects the contradictions of its moment of production'; and an attack on the literary critical process of discrimination of value which judges H 'as a great but deeply flawed writer'. This avowedly Marxist and deconstructionist study is interestingly provocative, but arid in manner and less original in its specific discussion of H's work than the large, theoretical claims might lead one to expect. H is also represented mainly by his novels, to the virtual exclusion of poems, short stories and *D*.

Under the Greenwood Tree

170   Danby, John F.
'Under the Greenwood Tree', *Critical Quarterly* 1:1 (Spring 1959) 5–13; reprinted in R. P. Draper (ed.), THOMAS HARDY: THREE PASTORAL NOVELS (91) 89–97

Explicit pessimism of later works is implicit in *UGT*. Time, as in *JO*, is the chief character here; it is the only solace and, while it brings grief, it bears it away. The comic resolution rests on the assumption that village life is eternal, but the bases of comedy are attacked by innovations which threaten the traditional village structure. Danby neatly describes the 'deciduous generations', the life of the community in a natural setting.

171   Draffan, Robert A.
'Hardy's *Under the Greenwood Tree*', *English* 22 (Summer 1973) 55–60

UGT can be seen as a sad book, at times cruel and unpleasant. The rustics are denigrated and exploited and there is a 'tainted quality' about the pastoral idyll. H's concept of women here is not heartening, and Dick is a fool, the object of H's 'gratuitous cruelty'. In spite of his later assertions in the Prefaces of *UGT*, H abandons the theme of the displaced choir in favour of the love story, and there is no sense of loss or sadness at its demise. (A refreshing, if over-stated, corrective to the traditional view of *UGT* as joyful idyll.)

172   Hands, Timothy
'Arthur Shirley (Vicar of Stinsford, 1837–91)', THOMAS HARDY ANNUAL No. 2, ed. Norman Page (London: Macmillan, 1984) 171–86

Shirley instigated an 'ecclesiastical revolution' in H's parish, and this is reflected in *UGT*'s portrayal of the parson.

173   Hardy, Barbara
        '*Under the Greenwood Tree:* A Novel about the
        Imagination', THE NOVELS OF THOMAS HARDY, ed.
        Anne Smith (London: Vision Press, 1979) 45–57

        Persuasive demonstration that all the characters in *UGT* are
        'active in the narrative forms of fantasy and memory',
        employing imagination to synthesise and particularise com-
        plex experience.

174   Howard, Jeanne
        'Thomas Hardy's "Mellstock" and the Registrar General's
        Stinsford', *Literature and History* 6 (Autumn 1977) 179–200

        The census of 1841 confirms the accuracy of H's portrayal of
        Stinsford in his fictional 'Mellstock', with its 'highly stratified
        rural community'. *UGT* shows a tension between the hist-
        orical and pastoral modes, between H's perception of radical
        change and his attempts to resolve it.

175   Kossick, S. G.
        '*Under the Greenwood Tree*', *Essays in Literature*,
        University of Denver 1 (January 1973) 30–4

        Fancy's marriage to Dick is a means of reinvigorating the old,
        but the novel does have its tragic elements and the comic
        ending cannot negate 'the sense of loss and dislocation'
        arising from the demise of the choir.

176   Page, Norman
        'Hardy's Dutch Painting: *Under the Greenwood Tree*',
        Thomas Hardy Year Book no. 5 (1975) 39–42. Reprinted in
        R. P. Draper (ed.), THOMAS HARDY: THREE
        PASTORAL NOVELS (91) 106–11

        The novel's subtitle (A Rural Painting of the Dutch School)
        indicates a pictorial and realistic study of the community, but
        H combines such realism with the mode of pastoral romance.
        He also evokes different pictorial traditions in his use of
        dramatic chiaroscuro effects or his portrayal of the Pre-
        Raphaelite Fancy Day. Page concludes this sensitive article
        with the opinion that 'Hardy's debts and analogues, pictorial

as well as literary, are more wide-ranging and complex than might be supposed'.

177 Toliver, Harold E.
'The Dance under the Greenwood Tree: Hardy's Bucolics', *Nineteenth-Century Fiction* 17:1 (June 1962) 57–68

The closing hints of discord between Fancy and Dick indicate the tenuous nature of the compromise between their two ways of life. Later novels show that those who abandon the simplicity of bucolic life for social or intellectual advance nearly always end unhappily. [Also discusses briefly the other major novels.]

Far from the Madding Crowd

178 Adey, Lionel
'Styles of Love in *Far from the Madding Crowd*', THOMAS
HARDY ANNUAL No. 5, ed. Norman Page (London:
Macmillan, 1987) 47–62

Rather cumbersome attempt to explore the modes or styles
in which the central characters of *FMC* express love, and to
what extent these 'result from or determine their attitude to
the land and its dependents'.

179 Babb, Howard
'Setting and Theme in *Far from the Madding Crowd*',
English Literary History 30 (June 1963) 147–61

The theme of *FMC* is the opposition between the natural and
the civilised, and the former is seen as much superior. The
natural setting reinforces this, acting in both realistic and
symbolic ways. Bathsheba's 'fundamental' affiliation to the
natural world makes her 'a rather artless woman' who is only
temporarily ensnared by the civilised world. This argument
seems highly debatable, as do Babb's ruminations on the
significance of the characters' names (Everdene 'can hardly
fail to echo *evergreen*') but otherwise this essay is sound and
perceptive.

180 Beatty, C. J. P.
'*Far from the Madding Crowd:* a Reassessment', THOMAS
HARDY AND THE MODERN WORLD (104) 14–36

Very detailed and stimulating evaluation of *FMC*, noting the
importance of architectural and geometric imagery.

181 Carpenter, Richard C.
'The Mirror and the Sword: Imagery in *Far from the
Madding Crowd*', *Nineteenth-Century Fiction* 18:4 (March
1964) 331–45

The patterns of images (colours, mirrors, clothing, swords) in this novel give it a musical design, the leitmotifs hinting especially at the nature of Bathsheba's sexuality and her desire to be dominated. The imagery gives a further dimension to *FMC*, making it not a mere melodramatic folktale but a powerful study of vanity, love and despair.

182   Casagrande, Peter J.
'A New View of Bathsheba Everdene', CRITICAL APPROACHES TO THE FICTION OF THOMAS HARDY, ed. Dale Kramer (London: Macmillan, 1979) 50–73

Revisionist view of Bathsheba as aggressively coy and an 'inadvertent, unconscious agent of evil'. H may sympathise with her infirmity but deplores her irrationality. Her lack of development at the end of the novel is shown in her motives for wanting to marry Oak: 'we find her doing what she had done earlier, seeking an environment in which she is the enshrined centre'. Casagrande's concentration on one character permits him to isolate H's often misogynist attitudes in *FMC*.

183   Chalfont, Fran E.
'From Strength to Strength: John Schlesinger's Film of *Far from the Madding Crowd*', THOMAS HARDY ANNUAL No. 5, ed. Norman Page (London: Macmillan, 1987) 63–74

Successful discussion of the 1967 film, pointing out many instances where it is arguably superior to the novel.

184   Drew, Elizabeth
'Thomas Hardy: *Far from the Madding Crowd*', THE NOVEL: A MODERN GUIDE TO FIFTEEN ENGLISH MASTERPIECES (New York: Norton, 1963) 141–55

Disappointing and conventional reading of *FMC*, defending the plot and showing how Oak is the symbolic ideal of a farmer. H, of course, was a 'gentle and humane soul'.

185   Elliott, Ralph, W. V.
A CRITICAL COMMENTARY ON THOMAS HARDY'S

FAR FROM THE MADDING CROWD (London: Macmillan, 1966)

Chapters on The Story, The Characters, etc. This is a conventional and derivative study.

186   Gatrell, Simon
'Hardy the Creator: *Far from the Madding Crowd*',
CRITICAL APPROACHES TO THE FICTION OF
THOMAS HARDY, ed. Dale Kramer (London:
Macmillan, 1979) 74–98

Analyses H's revisions to Chapters 40–43 of *FMC* to show changes in characterisation and social class and the kinds of interference and censorship from editors that prompted such changes. A scholarly and admirable account of H's textual practices.

187   Giordano, Frank R., Jr
'Farmer Boldwood: Hardy's Portrait of a Suicide', *English Literature in Transition* 21:4 (1978) 244–53

Enthusiastic and convincing argument that Boldwood has suicidal obsessions and is one of H's most successful male characters. Giordano draws on Durkheim and Freud to show H's precise and clinical portrayal. For dubious aesthetic reasons, H refused to let Boldwood kill himself.

188   Horne, Lewis
'Passion and Flood in *Far from the Madding Crowd*', *Ariel* 13 (1982) 39–49

Close reading of *FMC*, concentrating on the metaphors of water and flooding which represent passion in its various forms. Nature and emotion are closely intermingled, and neither is idealised in this novel which undermines 'the concept of a peaceful pastoral'.

189   Jones, Lawrence
'George Eliot and Pastoral Tragicomedy in Hardy's *Far from the Madding Crowd*', *Studies in Philology* 77 (1980) 402–25

Exceptionally clear and readable analysis of *FMC,* showing that H learned from *Adam Bede* 'how to combine pastoral realism with a strong plot that incorporates genuinely tragic elements and yet finally satisfies the "comic" demands of Victorian convention'. H adopts, modifies and pushes against the limits of this pattern; Eliot's pastoral tragicomedy served him well as a transition to his own form of tragedy.

190   Jones, Lawrence
'"A Good Hand at a Serial": Thomas Hardy and the Serialization of *Far from the Madding Crowd'*, *Studies in the Novel* 10 (Autumn 1978) 320–34

Demands of serial publication led H to compromise his aims in *FMC.* He increased elements of melodrama, sensation and suspense, and was careful not to offend sexual decorum. [Copious detail.]

191   Jones, Lawrence
'"Infected by a Vein of Mimeticism": George Eliot and the Technique of *Far from the Madding Crowd'*, *Journal of Narrative Technique* 8:1 (Winter 1978) 56–76

Shows Eliot's influence in H's use of 'static verbal pictures in the Dutch mode, in his use of block analyses of character, and in his use of scientific diction and metaphor and of self-conscious sententiousness in his omniscient analyses and commentary'.

192   Pettit, Charles P. C.
'Narrative Techniques in *Far from the Madding Crowd'*, *Thomas Hardy Society Review* 1:1 (1975) 16–27

Detailed study of H's limitation of perspectives which 'imaginatively exposes his perception of the essential isolation of the individual'. Echoes, contrasts, the rustic chorus and imagery all serve to unify the novel. A traditional but sensible analysis of *FMC.*

193   Reid, Fred
'Art and Ideology in *Far from the Madding Crowd'*,

THOMAS HARDY ANNUAL No. 4, ed. Norman Page
(London: Macmillan, 1986) 91–126

Densely argued and absorbing study, in part an historical and
contextual examination of *FMC*. Especially significant in its
analysis of Bathsheba, her marriage and the competing forms
of pastoral which the novel presents.

194   Schweik, Robert C.
'The Early Development of Hardy's *Far from the Madding
Crowd'*, *Texas Studies in Literature and Language* 9
(Autumn 1967) 415–28

Probes the early manuscript segment of *FMC* for evidence of
H's initial conception of the novel. It seems likely that the
roles of Fanny Robin and Boldwood were the results of late
revisions as H sought to complicate the conventional love
triangle with which he had begun. H was clearly seeking to
be more than merely a 'good hand at a serial'.

195   Schweik, Robert C.
'The Narrative Structure of *Far from the Madding Crowd'*,
BUDMOUTH ESSAYS ON THOMAS HARDY [etc. – see
103] 21–38

Thorough account of *FMC* shows that H's 'method of
composition was so thoroughly improvisatory' that 'the
resulting narrative structure is less a design than a record of
changing narrative strategies and expedients', especially with
regard to use of imagery, narrative focus and authorial
distance.

196   Shelston, Alan
'The Particular Pleasure of *Far from the Madding Crowd'*,
THOMAS HARDY YEAR BOOK, No. 7 (1977) 31–9.
Partly reprinted in R. P. Draper (ed.), THOMAS HARDY:
THREE PASTORAL NOVELS (91) 137–46

Excellent and enthusiastic account of *FMC*, stressing H's
'narrative security' and control in sustaining the tension
between the 'two fictional polarities' of the still permanence
of the natural world and the startling incidents of the
melodrama.

197 Slade, Tony
'Leslie Stephen and *Far from the Madding Crowd*', *Thomas Hardy Journal* 1:2 (May 1985) 31–40

Stephen's editorial scrutiny of the serialisation of *FMC* has usually been seen as commendable. Slade qualifies this by stressing Stephen's prudery, and desire for more action in the novel. Detailed examination of textual composition of *FMC*'s Chapter 23.

198 Squires, Michael
'*Far from the Madding Crowd* as Modified Pastoral', *Nineteenth-Century Fiction* 25:3 (December 1970) 299–326

FMC is, in part, a traditional pastoral novel, nostalgically stressing the beauty of its subject, but the many realistic details of rural life prevent falsification. 'Before the novel's essential realism, prettiness disappears.' [Excellent detailed study.]

199 Windram, William J.
'A Discrepancy in *Far from the Madding Crowd*', *Notes & Queries* ns. 29:4 (1982) 326

Gabriel is clearly twenty-eight years of age, but is Bathsheba six or eight years younger? The novel is inconsistent on this point.

The Return of the Native

200 Bailey, J. O.
'Temperament as Motive in *The Return of the Native*',
English Fiction in Transition 5:2 (1962) 21–9

Emphasises the responsibility of the characters and their
temperaments for their fates, as opposed to destiny.

201 Benvenuto, Richard
'Another Look at the Other Eustacia', *Novel* 4:1 (Autumn
1970) 77–9

Continues the debunking of Eustacia. H has doubts about
her rank individualism, 'not because her values are often
trivial, but because she takes her self as her primary source of
value'. Eustacia is a study in the nature of independence and
moral audacity.

202 Benvenuto, Richard
'*The Return of the Native* as a Tragedy in Six Books',
Nineteenth-Century Fiction 26:1 (June 1971) 83–93

Defends the ending of *RN*, for the comic conclusion serves
only to isolate Clym and make him tragic – 'his own tragic
victimizer'. Despite H's disclaimer before the start of the
final chapter, 'Clym is left precisely where Hardy's original
conception required him to be: in an indifferent and ambiguous world, searching to no apparent avail for what it is to do
well'.

203 Benway, Ann M. B.
'Oedipus Abroad: Hardy's Clym Yeobright and Lawrence's
Paul Morel', *Thomas Hardy Year Book* 13 (1986) 51–7

Clym and Paul (in *Sons and Lovers*) confront the obstacle of
an Oedipal attachment to their mothers. Unlike Paul, Clym
eventually 'chooses a living death' and an 'impotent
existence'.

204   Björk, Lennart A.
"'Visible Essences" as Thematic Structure in Hardy's *The Return of the Native'*, *English Studies* 53 (1972) 52–63

The principal 'visible essences' are Eustacia, representing the Hellenic view of life, and Clym, the man of the nineteenth century. Their irreconcilable opposition is an aesthetic and philosophical one which results in the eclipse of the Hellenic world's 'light, optimism, and luxuriance' by the 'philosophical resignation and emotional restraint' typical of Clym. Björk gives a sound portrayal of Clym but appears to distort Eustacia in order to establish this rather rigid antithesis.

205   Cohen, Sandy
'Blind Clym, Unchristian Christian and the Redness of the Reddleman: Character Correspondences in *The Return of the Native'*, THOMAS HARDY YEAR BOOK No. 11 (1984) 49–55

Traces some biblical correspondences. Diggory Venn may be seen as a Christ figure, though hardly a Messiah.

206   Crompton, Louis
'The Sunburnt God: Ritual and Tragic Myth in *The Return of the Native'*, *Boston University Studies in English* 4 (Winter 1960) 229–40

Clym and Eustacia are romantic and tragic figures who are also viewed as realistic characters in their subjection to the laws of biology and economics. They achieve a kind of mythical status while simultaneously being presented as 'insignificant figures' with little control over their fates.

207   Deen, Leonard W.
'Heroism and Pathos in Hardy's *Return of the Native'*, *Nineteenth-Century Fiction*, 15:3 (December 1960) 207–19; reprinted in R. P. Draper (ed.), HARDY: THE TRAGIC NOVELS (90) 119–32

On the nature of tragedy in *RN*. Focuses on Eustacia and, to a lesser extent, Clym. H does not control firmly the irony implicit in our double vision of Eustacia; *RN* begins heroically but slips into the diminishing ironic and pathetic mode of the later tragic novels. Clym is similarly a tragic figure reduced to a pitiable one. (Many acute comments, but Deen is unfortunately reluctant to answer his question whether these are 'legitimate' or 'peripheral' modes of tragedy.)

208   Eggenschwiler, David
'Eustacia Vye, Queen of Night and Courtly Pretender',
Nineteenth-Century Fiction 25:4 (March 1971) 444–54

Eustacia is both a silly dreamer and a tragic heroine. H's *intentionally* conflicting views of her show the complexity of his attitude to romanticism. Much of the 'heroic' rhetoric in the novel is actually mock-heroic. We thus have 'a double perspective on the romantic heroine'.

209   Emery, John P. and Weber, Carl J.
'Chronology in Hardy's *Return of the Native*', *PMLA* 54 (June 1939) 618–19, 620

Emery points out temporal inconsistencies and chronological errors in *RN*, and Weber replies to defend his earlier article (720). The classical unity of time is important in H's conception of tragedy in *RN*.

210   Evans, Robert
'The Other Eustacia', *Novel* 1 (Spring 1968) 251–9

H tried to make Eustacia a tragic heroine, but there is another Eustacia in the novel who appears as merely an adolescent and selfish girl. H fails to fuse these two Eustacias and so he creates only a 'pseudo-tragic figure' who frustrates the reader led to expect a tragedy. Compare Eggenschwiler's view (208) that such ambiguity is deliberate and controlled. See also Benvenuto (201).

211   Fleishman, Avrom
'The Buried Giant of Egdon Heath: An Archaeology of Folklore in *The Return of the Native*', FICTION AND THE WAYS OF KNOWING: ESSAYS ON BRITISH NOVELS (Austin and London: University of Texas Press, 1978) 110–22

Fascinating study of the mythological and folkloric contexts of the heath, seeing it as subdued ogre, bound Titan and a 'third type of giant not so much rebellious as long-suffering, dormant but expectant'. The heath 'carries, among its many resonances of power and endurance, a vibration not so much stoical as regenerative and creative – whatever the failure of its denizens to make much of their connections with it'.

212 Gindin, James (ed.)
THOMAS HARDY: *THE RETURN OF THE NATIVE:* AN AUTHORITATIVE TEXT, BACKGROUND, CRITICISM, Norton Critical Editions (New York: Norton, 1969)

Useful edition which includes reviews and more recent criticism of the novel.

213 Giordano, Frank R., Jr
'Eustacia Vye's Suicide', *Texas Studies in Literature and Language* 30 (1980) 504–21

Re-examines Eustacia's death in the light of her self-destructive temperament, arguing that 'the thematic structure of the novel as well as the evolution of Eustacia's fundamentally Pagan character require that she commit suicide'.

214 Gose, Elliott B., Jr
'*The Return of the Native*', IMAGINATION INDULGED: THE IRRATIONAL IN THE NINETEENTH CENTURY NOVEL (Montreal: McGill-Queens University Press, 1972) 95–125 et seq.

In *RN,* H presents an archetypal frame of reference by means of ritual, romance, folklore and primitive rhythms which integrate nature, the peasants and Eustacia. *RN* gives us a credible fairy-tale embodying universal psychological processes.

215 Hagan, John
'A Note on the Significance of Diggory Venn', *Nineteenth-Century Fiction* 16:2 (September 1961) 147–55

Surveys previous critical opinion of Venn, that pivotal and exceedingly strange character. Synthesises such views by showing he is both Satanic and good: 'This incongruity itself is the key: in the unintentional devilishness of both his appearance and the effects of his actions, on the one hand, combined with the basic goodness of his heart and will, on the other, is epitomized that fundamental awryness of things . . . which is the ultimate fact about the universe of the novel.'

216   Hanley, Katherine
'Death as Option: The Heroine in Nineteenth-Century Fiction', *College Language Association Journal* 25:2 (1981) 197–202

On the ambiguities of Eustacia's suicide. Comparisons with other female suicides in fiction.

217   Heilman, Robert B.
'*The Return:* Centennial Observations', THE NOVELS OF THOMAS HARDY, ed. Anne Smith (London: Vision Press, 1979) 58–90

Broad and generous tribute to *RN,* concentrating on narrative structure and style and stressing its anticipation of the later work.

218   Hopkins, V.T.
'Clym the Obscure', *Thomas Hardy Society Review* 1:9 (1983) 273–5

Clym is a forerunner of Jude: both are clever young men with high ideals. Clym, however, never 'justifies the build-up given him' and he is the least successful of H's major characters. As an 'obscure dot among the foliage', Clym is 'the lonely face of Egdon', closer to St Francis than to John the Baptist.

219   Johnson, S. F.
'Hardy and Burke's "Sublime"', STYLE IN PROSE FICTION: ENGLISH INSTITUTE ESSAYS 1958, ed. Harold C. Martin (New York: Columbia University Press, 1959) 55–86

Edmund Burke's *Enquiry into the Sublime and Beautiful* seems to have been almost a handbook for H in the writing of *RN,* which utilises many of Burke's sources of sublimity in literature (terror, infirmity, pain, power, vastness).

220 Jordan, M. E.
'Thomas Hardy's *The Return of the Native:* Clym Yeobright and Melancholia', *American Imago* 39 (1982) 101–18

'Psychological' reading of *RN.*

221 Kramer, Dale
'Unity of Time in *The Return of the Native*', *Notes & Queries* 210 (August 1965), 304–5

H observes the dramatic unity of time by making *RN*'s action last a year and three days. In a description of Egdon Heath, he shows how a human year is but a day in nature's reckoning (Book IV, Ch. I). H's classical unity thus provides an 'ironic, ego-deflating gloss upon time'.

222 Litz, A. Walton
'Introduction', THE RETURN OF THE NATIVE (New York: Houghton Mifflin, 1967) v–xv

H needed a traditional form in order to integrate the 'old illusions' of the ballads with his own age's 'new alignment'. He found it in classical tragedy (*RN*'s tragic conventions are described), yet H fails to create a suitably tragic Clym, who is merely a 'pathetic figure'. Eustacia, in contrast, is compelling, the main source of *RN*'s 'extraordinary power over our imaginations'.

223 Martin, Bruce K.
'Whatever Happened to Eustacia Vye?', *Studies in the Novel* 4:4 (Winter 1972) 619–27

Alternative interpretations of Eustacia's death as suicide, pure accident or accidental but self-willed can all be sustained. However, H did not specify the cause of death because he wished to downgrade her importance in the novel and stress instead Clym's role as protagonist. The dramatic crisis resulting from suicide or accidental death would have interfered with H's wish to switch protagonists in midstream, which is a structural flaw in the novel.

224   Murphree, A. A. and Strauch, C. F.
'The Chronology of *The Return of the Native*', *Modern Language Notes* 54 (November 1939) 491–7

Disputes Weber's assertion (719) that H wrote *RN* with a calendar of 1842 in front of him; if he did, H 'quite lost sight of the calendar' on many occasions. H was not the schematic and architectonic novelist whom Weber depicted.

225   Paterson, John (ed.)
'Introduction', THE RETURN OF THE NATIVE (New York: Harper & Row, 1966) ix–xxviii. Partly reprinted in R. P. Draper (ed.), HARDY: THE TRAGIC NOVELS (90) 109–18

Important 'poetic' defence of *RN* which, viewed as a tragedy, is pretentious and ludicrous. The novel survives the defects of the plot because of 'the greater and more inclusive music of theme and imagery', especially its irradiating Promethean imagery of bonfires and burning sun. *RN*'s subversive anti-Christian argument was driven underground by the censorship of the day, but much of the novel's power derives from the fact that H was compelled 'to dramatize indirectly, at the level of artistic suggestion, what he couldn't plainly say'.

226   Paterson, John
THE MAKING OF *THE RETURN OF THE NATIVE* (Berkeley and Los Angeles: University of California Press, 1960)

Masterly account of *RN*'s development from the 'equivalent of a rough draft' to the Wessex edition. The setting in pastoral Wessex is widened, Eustacia becomes less Satanic and more Byronic, Diggory ascends to the middle classes and Wildeve is made to appear younger. The finished novel is 'quite as much the product of revision as the product of vision'.

227 Paterson, John
'The "Poetics" of *The Return of the Native*', *Modern Fiction Studies* 6 (Autumn 1960) 214–22

Discusses classical influences on *RN*. Like a Greek tragedy, the novel is limited in time and place. The peasants serve as a kind of chorus. The text is virtually saturated with the Promethean motif and fire imagery. By such means does H place the otherwise purely local action of the novel within a frame of dignified and significant reference.

228 Paterson, John
'*The Return of the Native* as Antichristian Document', *Nineteenth-Century Fiction* 14:2 (September 1959) 11–27

RN 'dramatizes the tragic humiliation, in the diminished world of the modern consciousness, of an heroic, prechristian understanding'. Eustacia, Diggory Venn and the peasant chorus serve to make *RN* an 'anticlerical tract' which commemorates 'in an elegiac if not tragic mood, the defeat of pagan consciousness and the triumph of Christian conscience'.
   Clym's conversion at the end of *RN* makes him a mediocre and ironic figure of Christian piety.

229 Ray, Martin
'Hardy's Borrowing from Shakespeare: Eustacia Vye and Lady Macbeth', *Thomas Hardy Year Book* 14 (1987) 64

Shakespearean allusions in *RN* suggest that H is regarding Eustacia at times as 'a kind of Lady Macbeth figure', a worldly and ambitious woman. Their respective deaths (possibly suicide) have a similar ambiguity.

230 Schweik, Robert C.
'Theme, Character, and Perspective in Hardy's *The Return of the Native*', *Philological Quarterly* 41 (October 1962) 757–67

In *RN*, H examines the validity of certain kinds of insight and outlook, each represented by a different character. Eustacia embodies the 'sensuous paganism' of the past, Mrs Yeobright the practical conventionality of the present, and Clym the 'thoughtful asceticism of the future'. The insight of each is, however, severely limited by temperament and circumstances.

231   Southerington, F. R.
        '*The Return of the Native:* Thomas Hardy and the Evolution of Consciousness', THOMAS HARDY AND THE MODERN WORLD (104) 37–47

Philosophic account of H's study of sensitive consciousness in an insensitive, indifferent world; man's place may be at the summit of his world, but his eminence is useful to him only in the service of others, his vision limited, and his command of the future at best uncertain. 'What is focused upon here is the futility of a self-asserting will to enjoy in the face of the astonishing *slowness* of time.'

232   Wheeler, Otis B.
        'Four Versions of *The Return of the Native*', *Nineteenth-Century Fiction* 14:1 (June 1959) 27–44

Scholarly account of the seven stages in the novel's development, showing how H's revisions made the characters more plausible, the conflicts stronger and the plot more tightly knit.

233   Zellefrow, Ken
        '*The Return of the Native:* Hardy's Map and Eustacia's Suicide', *Nineteenth-Century Fiction* 28:2 (September 1973) 214–20

Plausible case that Eustacia's death is a deliberate and tragic suicide rather than an accidental drowning.

The Mayor of Casterbridge

234   Aschkenasy, Nehama
       'Biblical Substructures in the Tragic Form: Hardy, *The
       Mayor of Casterbridge*, Agnon, *And the Crooked Shall Be
       Made Straight*', *Modern Language Studies* 13:1 (1983)
       101–10

       Comparison of the two novels, which are both said to be
       saturated with scriptural citations. For instance, Henchard
       and Farfrae enact the Saul–David conflict. Also discusses
       Henchard as Oedipus.

235   Brown, Douglas
       HARDY: *THE MAYOR OF CASTERBRIDGE,* Studies in
       English Literature Series (London: Edward Arnold; New
       York: Barron's Educational Series, 1962)

       Guide to the novel for the advanced student and under-
       graduate. Aimed at a more sophisticated reader than Unwin's
       guide (260). Gives a thorough, chapter-by-chapter analysis of
       MC, focusing especially on the rivalry between Henchard and
       Farfrae and the defeat of the old rural system by the new
       technology.

236   Dike, D. A.
       'A Modern Oedipus: *The Mayor of Casterbridge*', *Essays in
       Criticism* 2 (April 1952) 169–79

       Henchard's conflict with Farfrae resembles that between
       Oedipus and Creon and also 'the sacred combat between the
       old god, priest, or father and the new'. Market forces replace
       fate and determine their destinies. This is an important
       article in that it stresses the novel's debt to classical tragedy
       and ritual, but it pursues its thesis rather immoderately.

237   Dollar, J. Gerard
       'The "Looped Orbit" of the Mayor of Casterbridge', *Papers
       on Language and Literature* 19:3 (Summer 1983) 293–308

'The conflict between centripetal and centrifugal forces, the unwilled return and the will to move on, results in a paradoxical "circling forward", and it is this movement, above all, which characterizes Michael Henchard's career.' Pessimistic reading of *MC* which sees H as withholding even the consolation that death represents an escape from the circularity of time.

238   Draper, R. P.
       'The Mayor of Casterbridge', Critical Quarterly 25:1 (Spring 1983) 57–70

Draper argues that the novel shows a shift from an Aristotelian to a more Schopenhauerian form of tragedy; though H 'does not cause the one to cancel out the other, but allows the two to co-exist in a tension which is both heroic and disenchanted'.

239   Edmond, Rod
       ' "The Past-marked Prospect": *The Mayor of Casterbridge',* READING THE VICTORIAN NOVEL: DETAIL INTO FORM, ed. Ian Gregor (London: Vision Press, 1980) 111–27

Very detailed study of *MC*, in which 'issues of the past, of history and memory' have their most concentrated expression in H's fiction. Proceeds to a more affective analysis of how time is experienced by the reader of a novel 'written in the 1880s, about the 1840s, which begins in the 1820s'.

240   Edwards, Duane D.
       'The Mayor of Casterbridge as Aeschylean Tragedy', *Studies in the Novel,* 4:4 (Winter 1972) 608–18

MC shows the same relationship between past and present as Aeschylus does in his tragedies. The inevitability of Henchard's fate derives not from the wife-sale but from its combination with later, indeterminate events. Interesting on H's use of a subjective narrator limited in perception.

241   Grindle, Juliet M.
       'Compulsion and Choice in *The Mayor of Casterbridge',*

THE NOVELS OF THOMAS HARDY, ed. Anne Smith
(London: Vision Press, 1979) 91–106

Acute and readable study of power and different kinds of
mastery in *MC*, especially Henchard's attempt to control
relationships as if they were financial debts to be repaid. The
metaphors which associate Henchard initially with bulls and
then with the caged bird show the changing status he enjoys
and his responses to his reducing power.

242   Haig, Stirling
       ' "By the Rivers of Babylon": Water and Exile in *The
       Mayor of Casterbridge'*, *Thomas Hardy Year Book* 11 (1984)
       55–64

Traces the novel's motifs of water, downfall, death and
foreignness to show its preoccupation with 'instability and
fluidity'. The central characters, far from achieving 'fixity and
identity', are portrayed 'in a constant state of suspension
marked by fluidity and rootlessness'.

243   Heilman, Robert B.
       'Hardy's *Mayor*: Notes on Style', *Nineteenth-Century Fiction*
       18:4 (March 1964) 307–29

Detailed close reading shows that the problem of H's style is
its inconsistency, varying between the concrete and the
muddled, or the untutored and the quasi-classical.

244   Jones, Myrddin
       'Hardy and Biblical Narrative', *Thomas Hardy Society
       Newsletter* no. 60 (1984) 9–11

Illustrates H's admiration of the Bible's stories, with special
reference to *MC* and the parallels between Henchard and
Cain. Jones offers further corroboration of this thesis in his
'Hardy and Biblical Narrative', *Thomas Hardy Journal* 1:1
(1985) 24.

245   Karl, Frederick R.
       '*The Mayor of Casterbridge*: A New Fiction Defined',
       Modern Fiction Studies 6 (Autumn 1960) 195–213.

Reprinted in MODERN BRITISH FICTION: ESSAYS IN CRITICISM, ed. Mark Schorer (New York: Oxford University Press, 1961) 10–29. Reprinted and supplemented, with the same title, in *Modern Fiction Studies* 21 (1975) 405–28

Sees Henchard as a 'new type of nineteenth-century man', a split individual ruled by a mysterious universe and a misdirected will. H's realism in *MC* extends beyond the social realism of Dickens, Eliot and Thackeray and presents a psychological history. Henchard is denied the traditional salvation of recovery after penance. [Karl's 1975 commentary, pp 424–8, stresses the extent to which H foreshadows Kafka's 'claustrophobic reality'. Henchard represents a vision of a being self-enclosed.]

246   Karl, Frederick R.
'Thomas Hardy's "Mayor" and the Changing Novel', AN AGE OF FICTION: THE NINETEENTH CENTURY BRITISH NOVEL (New York: Farrar, Straus & Giroux, 1964) 295–322; reprinted as A READER'S GUIDE TO THE NINETEENTH CENTURY BRITISH NOVEL (New York: Noonday Press, 1965) 295–322

Revises and slightly expands Karl's 1960 article on *MC*.

247   Kiely, Robert
'Vision and Viewpoint in *The Mayor of Casterbridge*', *Nineteenth-Century Fiction* 23:2 (September 1968) 189–200

MC includes 'some of the busiest amateur spies in serious fiction'. The novel's central concern is the way people look at themselves and one another. H extends the artist's preoccupation with perspective to a larger philosophical preoccupation with self-knowledge and moral choice, and characters 'experience their most significant crises in terms of vision rather than action'. (Especially good on Henchard's failure to 'adjust his perspective'. Extensive discussion also of Lucetta and the chorus.)

248   Kramer, Dale
'Character and the Cycle of Change in *The Mayor of Casterbridge*', *Tennessee Studies in Literature* 16 (1971) 111–20

On the structural complexity of *MC*. H regarded history as both cyclical and as a 'looped orbit' which may permit progress. Farfrae may seem to be an example of successful adaptation, but he is flawed and can in turn be supplanted.

249   Lerner, Laurence
THOMAS HARDY'S *THE MAYOR OF CASTERBRIDGE*: TRAGEDY OR SOCIAL HISTORY? (London: Chatto & Windus, for Sussex University Press, 1975)

This book belongs to a series entitled 'Text and Context'. Lerner places *MC* in three such contexts: the literary context of other novels by Zola and Jeffries dealing with comparable material; the philosophical context, involving Schopenhauer, Darwin and theorists of tragedy; and the social context, involving economic and sociological changes. Lerner's conclusion is that none of these contexts is sufficient in itself; for a proper appreciation of the novel all three must be taken into account: 'When treating *The Mayor* as tragedy, or as cosmic statement, we ought not to lose sight of the actuality of Casterbridge . . . When treating it as a social novel, we ought not to shut our ears to the way it is like Shakespeare, to the timeless grandeur of Henchard, and to the fact that it offers constant parallels, structural and emotional, to very different works about very different societies.'

250   McBride, Mary G.
'The Influence of *On Liberty* on Thomas Hardy's *The Mayor of Casterbridge*', *Mill News Letter* 19:1 (Winter 1984) 12–17

MC includes a number of specific illustrations which also appear in Mill's work. More significantly, 'the concept of individualism in Mill's essay provides a philosophic context for the tragic themes manifested in the character of Michael Henchard'.

251   Maxwell, J. C.
'The "Sociological" Approach to *The Mayor of Casterbridge*', IMAGINED WORLDS: ESSAYS ON SOME ENGLISH NOVELS AND NOVELISTS IN HONOUR OF JOHN BUTT, ed. Ian Gregor and Maynard

Mack (London: Methuen, 1968) 225–36. Partly reprinted in
R. P. Draper (ed.) HARDY: THE TRAGIC NOVELS (90)
48–57

Maxwell throws doubt on the historical accuracy of critics
like Douglas Brown (117), who suggests that *MC* is about the
agricultural collapse of the late nineteenth century. Rather,
Henchard should be seen as an exceptional character in a
time of stability. Maxwell also opposes the idea of a simple
contrast between Henchard and Farfrae as old-style and
new-style businessmen.

252   Paterson, John
'Hardy, Faulkner, and the Prosaics of Tragedy', *Centennial
Review* 5 (Spring 1961) 156–75

Sees *MC* as a tragedy where plot dominates character, even
Henchard's masterful personality. Even the realistic elements
of *MC* are 'assimilated by the tragic structure of the novel'.
While Paterson is keen to show that *MC* is a tragedy, and
invokes comparisons with Oedipus and Lear to promote this
argument, he does not succeed in showing how *MC* is a tragic
novel.

253   Paterson, John
'*The Mayor of Casterbridge* as Tragedy', *Victorian Studies* 3
(December 1959) 151–72; reprinted in Albert J. Guerard
(ed.) (93) 91–112

MC is seen as traditional tragedy 'in its olden, in its
Sophoclean or Shakespearean, sense', with Henchard being
punished for the sale of his wife by a supernatural power.
Paterson applauds the novel's archaic and anachronistic
status, as he defines it, and ignores the extent to which
characters determine their own fate.

254   Pinion, F. B.
A CRITICAL COMMENTARY ON THOMAS HARDY'S
THE MAYOR OF CASTERBRIDGE (London: Macmillan,
1966)

Wide-ranging survey of *MC*, discussing many aspects (e.g.
the presentation of the story, literary influences, serialisation,
setting).

255 Robinson, James K. (ed.)
THE MAYOR OF CASTERBRIDGE: AN
AUTHORITATIVE TEXT, BACKGROUNDS,
CRITICISM, Norton Critical Editions (New York: Norton,
1977)

This edition appends background material on setting, composition, publication and reviews; comments by H; selections of recent criticism of the novel.

256 Schweik, Robert C.
'Character and Fate in Hardy's *The Mayor of Casterbridge'*,
Nineteenth-Century Fiction 21:3 (December 1966) 249–62;
reprinted in R. P. Draper (ed.), HARDY: THE TRAGIC
NOVELS (90) 133–47

Excellent attempt to account for the 'deliberate' inconsistencies in H's portrayal of Henchard. In the first half of *MC*, there seems to be a 'fable-like correspondence of fate and character' so that his moral stature runs parallel to his economic fortunes, and his moral offence is followed by just retribution. Later, however, something less than ideal justice governs the 'grim irony of events'. The second half disproves the opening fable that the good shall prosper and the wicked fail, as we see a repentant Henchard increasingly frustrated in his acts of expiation and brought to suffer disproportionately.

257 Showalter, Elaine
'The Unmanning of the Mayor of Casterbridge', CRITICAL
APPROACHES TO THE FICTION OF THOMAS
HARDY, ed. Dale Kramer (London: Macmillan, 1979)
99–115

Feminist and sympathetic study of Henchard: his efforts, 'first to deny and divorce his passional self, and ultimately to accept and educate it, involve him in a pilgrimage of "unmanning" which is a movement towards both self-discovery and tragic vulnerability'. Henchard thus becomes a New Man, acquiring the 'feminine' skills of 'observation, attention, sensitivity, and compassion'.

258   Starzyk, Lawrence J.
'Hardy's *Mayor*: The Antitraditional Basis of Tragedy',
Studies in the Novel 4:4 (Winter 1972) 592–607

To regard *MC* as a traditional tragedy requires the presence
of a transcendent moral order, but the novel repeatedly and
rebelliously denies its existence. Suffering seems the sole
principle in H's conception of tragedy.

259   Taft, Michael
'Hardy's Manipulation of Folklore and Literary Imagination:
The Case of the Wife-Sale in *The Mayor of Casterbridge*',
Studies in the Novel 13:4 (Winter 1981) 399–407

H drew on a newspaper account of a wife-sale, but he may
also have known a popular broadside ballad on the subject.

260   Unwin, G. G.
THE MAYOR OF CASTERBRIDGE, Notes on English
Literature Series (Oxford: Basil Blackwell; New York:
Barnes & Noble, 1964)

A guide to the novel for students. Eighty pages contain seven
chapters with rather old-fashioned titles such as Style and
Plot, Characters and Themes. Detailed analysis of the novel's
Chapter 39 (the skimmity-ride). Each chapter ends with
suggested essay titles. A useful book, especially helpful in
schools.

261   Winfield, Christine
'Factual Sources of Two Episodes in *The Mayor of
Casterbridge*', *Nineteenth-Century Fiction* 25:2 (September
1970) 224–31

The sale of Henchard's wife and child and his bankruptcy
hearing were suggested to H by his reading of local newspapers of the 1820s.

The Woodlanders

262   Austin, Frances
'Dialogue in *The Woodlanders*', *Thomas Hardy Society Review* 1:5 (1979) 144–51

Interesting account of who uses dialect in *W*. Giles, a rustic, speaks standard English because the dignity of tragedy demands it.

263   Bayley, John
'A Social Comedy? On Re-reading *The Woodlanders*', THOMAS HARDY ANNUAL No. 5, ed. Norman Page (London: Macmillan, 1987) 3–21

W is H's most 'undercover novel' whose ultimate foundation is social comedy, demonstrating that 'sex and class, and all that they bring in the way of obsession and possession, can be seen in the end as a comedy that is grim, certainly, but not so grim as all that'. For instance, this is the only H novel in which a husband and wife get along moderately well together, surviving 'by means of life's small comforts and compensations, in the midst of general and accepted unsatisfactoriness'. Grace at the end 'disappears into the monotonies of living', confirming the sense of the novel as 'predominantly a comedy of small things, and very honest ones'.

264   Casagrande, Peter J.
'The Shifted "Centre of Altruism" in *The Woodlanders*: Thomas Hardy's Third "Return of a Native"', *Journal of English Literary History* 38 (March 1971) 104–25

W, conceived in the 1870s, is compared to *UGT* and *RN* as a 'return' fable. The latter two are respectively comic and tragic, while *W* has an ironic view of nature strongly influenced by Darwinian thought. H's several 'return' novels, including *MC*, *T* and *JO*, 'embody in their very structures the central experience of his life and art – the relationship of the old and the new, of the past and the present'.

265   Chalfont, Fran C.
        'In Defence of Hardy's Gentleman from South Carolina',
        Thomas Hardy Society Review 1:5 (1979) 142–4

        The passionate American who shoots Felice Charmond and
        kills himself is yet another of the novel's tragedies of the
        unfulfilled.

266   Diskin, Patrick
        'Joyce's "The Dead" and Hardy's *The Woodlanders*', *Notes
        & Queries*, ns. 30:4 (1983) 330–1

        The self-sacrifice of Giles in *W* which leads to his death is
        said to have influenced the ending of Joyce's 'The Dead',
        where Gretta's young lover dies of exposure. Some close
        verbal parallels are produced in evidence.

267   Drake, Robert Y.
        '*The Woodlanders* as Traditional Pastoral', *Modern Fiction
        Studies* 6 (Autumn 1960) 251–7

        'Pastoral' is not a term of abuse but a major tradition which
        embraces the duality of the natural world and the human
        heart. *W*'s conflict is between pastoral love ('traditional') and
        anti-pastoral love ('modernism'). At the conclusion of the
        novel, Grace refuses to renounce her Arcadian principles,
        but Fitzpiers, significantly, does modify his modernist
        opinions.

268   Essex, Ruth
        'A New Sentimental Journey', *Thomas Hardy Society
        Review* 1:9 (1983) 285–7

        This is a character study of Felice Charmond which tries to
        be more charitable to her than her creator apparently was.
        Makes the interesting point that *W* 'is unique in that the
        secondary female character foreshadows and parallels the
        development and actions of the heroine. The younger Grace
        has many of the values which have become second nature to
        the older Felice.'

269 Forster, E. M.
'Woodlanders on Devi', *New Statesman and Nation* 17
(6 May 1939) 679–80

Interesting account of reading *W* in India: 'Trees, trees,
undergrowth, English trees! How that book rustles with
them!'

270 Giordano, Frank R., Jr
'The Martyrdom of Giles Winterborne', THOMAS
HARDY ANNUAL No. 2, ed. Norman Page (London:
Macmillan, 1984) 61–78

An unusual Freudian view of Giles as a suicidal character
who brings his troubles on himself. He is noble, but an
ineffective lover. He displaces rather than vents his anger;
'his self-reproaches are reproaches against Grace, which have
been shifted back upon himself', and he feels 'unconscious
hatred' towards her for having abandoned him.

271 Greiff, Louis K.
'Symbolic Action in Hardy's *The Woodlanders*: An
Application of Burkian Theory', *Thomas Hardy Year Book*
14 (1987) 52–62

Analyses the scene at Giles' hut, leading to his death, and
proposes that here, symbolically, H is proposing that natural
marriage (such as that enjoyed by Grace and Giles) is an
attractive alternative to institutional marriage. They have a
rich, if temporary, relationship in this scene of 'unregulated
life'. Her eventual return to her husband shows H's view of
marriage as tragic yet inevitable.

272 Higgins, Lesley
'"Strange webs of melancholy": Shelleyan Echoes in *The
Woodlanders*', THOMAS HARDY ANNUAL No. 5, ed.
Norman Page (London: Macmillan, 1987) 38–46

Traces allusions to Shelley in *W* to show how H deliberately
uses Shelley to define '"the ache of modernism".'

273   Irvin, Glenn
       'Structure and Tone in *The Woodlanders*', THOMAS
       HARDY ANNUAL No. 2, ed. Norman Page (London:
       Macmillan, 1984) 79–90

       Irvin sees *W* as a comedy crossed with pathos and tragic
       irony, based on 'a socio-economic and educational issue'.
       The old order gives way to the new, and this is endorsed by
       the novel's structure, but the tone is one of regret for the
       passing of the old and contempt for the new.

274   Jacobus, Mary
       'Tree and Machine: *The Woodlanders*', CRITICAL
       APPROACHES TO THE FICTION OF THOMAS
       HARDY, ed. Dale Kramer (London: Macmillan, 1979)
       116–34

       Partly a contextual study, placing *W* in relation to topical
       cultural and intellectual ideas. The novel is an elegy for a lost
       mythology of nature invaded by predators from the modern
       world, by science and man-traps. In place of organic renewal
       and seasonal cycles, there are only compromises and contri-
       vances. Jacobus is especially interesting on the novel's
       serialisation and on its relation to pastoral.

275   Kramer, Dale
       'Revisions and Vision: Thomas Hardy's *The Woodlanders*',
       Bulletin of the New York Public Library 75 (April–May
       1971) 195–282

       Comprehensive study of H's extensive revisions over twenty-
       five years.

276   Lodge, David
       '*The Woodlanders*: A Darwinian Pastoral Elegy',
       WORKING WITH STRUCTURALISM: ESSAYS AND
       REVIEWS ON NINETEENTH- AND TWENTIETH-
       CENTURY LITERATURE (London: Routledge & Kegan
       Paul, 1981) 79–94. An abridged version of Lodge's
       Introduction to the New Wessex edition of *W* (1)

       Stresses the 'delicate, precarious balance' which H main-
       tained between the conventions of pastoral elegy and 'the
       new evolutionary account of the biological world'.

277 Matchett, William H.
'*The Woodlanders*, or Realism in Sheep's Clothing',
Nineteenth-Century Fiction 9:4 (March 1955) 241–61

Describes in detail how H, in *W*, attempts to express his pessimistic view of reality within the sentimental literary conventions of serial fiction. The result is not entirely successful, but H's sincerity ensures that the novel gives a tenable view of reality and necessary unhappiness.

278 Peck, John
'Hardy's *The Woodlanders*: The Too Transparent Web',
English Literature in Transition 24:3 (1981) 147–54

H is too explicit in his language and his series of connections and correspondences within the novel, which thus lacks the ability of his other major works to suggest the uncertainty of life.

279 Thesing, William B.
' "The Question of Matrimonial Divergence": Distorting Mirrors and Windows in Hardy's *The Woodlanders*',
Thomas Hardy Year Book 14 (1987) 44–52

Traces the two patterns of imagery pertaining to windows and mirrors to show how these 'distorting instruments' work against fulfilment of personal relationships, and develop *W*'s theme of delusion and immature vision. Characters repeatedly rely upon limited, glimpsed or framed perspectives, deceiving themselves and others.

Tess of the d'Urbervilles

280   Adamson, Jane
'*Tess of the d'Urbervilles*: Time and its Shapings', *Critical Review* 26 (1984) 18–36

Outlines H's twin interest in 'time's shaping pressures and in the scope or room for manoeuvre that a human consciousness finds within them'. This ambiguous relationship is finally unresolvable.

281   Bill, Judith R.
'The "Golden" World in *Tess of the d'Urbervilles*', *Thomas Hardy Society Review* 1:10 (1984) 307–10

H's landscapes in *T* may often be grey and cold, but he did create two other worlds (the valley of the Var and the 'golden' environment of the Trantridge cottagers and Marlott fieldworkers) which are vibrant, fertile and warm. The cottagers and fieldworkers 'inhabit a golden world, ruled by the sun and his subaltern the moon', and H shows how a socialised Christianity has tarnished this 'more natural, pre-civilized religious time'. At the end, significantly the sun shines on the altar of Stonehenge and allows Tess to rest in comfort and peace.

282   Blake, Kathleen
'Pure Tess: Hardy on Knowing a Woman', *Studies in English Literature 1500–1900* 22 (1982) 689–705

Thorough and detailed essay, showing how Tess 'inspires art by the same token that she suffers misapprehension and misuse'. *T* is the best embodiment of H's ideas 'about knowledge of the beautiful and the beloved'. Includes useful survey of critical approaches to Tess.

283   Bonica, Charlotte
'Nature and Paganism in Hardy's *Tess of the d'Urbervilles*', *Journal of English Literary History* 49 (1982) 849–62

Argues forcibly that H did not seek to suggest that 'the pagan relationship with nature offers modern individuals a useful replacement for Christianity' or a balm against modernism. On the contrary, he shows that 'the natural world, particularly through its inexorable sexual force, displays cruelty and injustice'.

284   Brady, Kristin
'Tess and Alec: Rape or Seduction?', THOMAS HARDY ANNUAL No. 4, ed. Norman Page (London: Macmillan, 1986) 127–47

Even to pose this perennial question, Brady suggests, shows the reductive thinking about sex, especially in H's audience. The scene in the Chase is left deliberately opaque and ambivalent, highlighting 'the complexity and the contradictoriness' of Tess's sexual responsiveness.

285   Brick, Allan
'Paradise and Consciousness in Hardy's *Tess*', *Nineteenth-Century Fiction* 17:2 (September 1962) 115–34

A copious analysis of the imagery of Eden and the fall in *T* shows the tension between a naïve idealism and a 'real' world inimical to any affirmation.

286   Brown, Suzanne Hunter
' "Tess" and *Tess*: An Experiment in Genre', *Modern Fiction Studies* 28:1 (Spring 1982) 25–44

Takes a scene in *T* (the death of the horse) and interprets it as if it were a self-contained short story, showing how readers have quite different critical assumptions and expectations for different genres. Does not reveal very much about H's novel.

287   'A chat with Mr. Hardy', BOOK BUYER, ns. 9 (May 1892) 153

Important interview with H, in which he discusses Tess who, he says, remained pure until her last fall when ' "she was as a mere corpse drifting in the water to her end – an absolutely irresponsible being".'

288   Claridge, Laura
       'Tess: A Less than Pure Woman Ambivalently Presented',
       Texas Studies in Literature and Language 28:3 (Fall 1986)
       324–37

       Argues that H tried to present Tess as a heroine commanding
       the reader's unqualified sympathy but there are 'too many
       cross currents that undermine his intention'. Images and
       allusions reveal a sub-text in which Tess shows some 'com-
       plicity in her fate' and Alec is less the villain than appears on
       the surface. 'It is Hardy the master of dark poetic truths who
       speaks so persuasively throughout this novel, and it is Hardy
       the novelist who works *against* his own text.'

289   Daleski, H. M.
       '*Tess of the d'Urbervilles*: Mastery and Abandon', *Essays in
       Criticism* 30 (1980) 326–45

       A welcome assertion that 'it is as a responsible tragic agent –
       not helpless victim – that we should view' Tess. Her tragedy
       lies in 'her own failure to integrate flesh and spirit'; for
       instance, her love for Angel is a 'flight from flesh', in that she
       idealises him and represses her passion, and in their love 'the
       flesh is as surely and mutually denied as is the spirit in her
       relationship with Alec'. She is tragic because 'it is she who
       has torn her life to pieces' by wanting Angel but giving
       herself to Alec. This is a wide-ranging general discussion of
       the novel, refreshing in its unsentimental and unpatronising
       view of Tess.

290   Eakins, Rosemary L.
       'Tess: The Pagan and Christian Traditions', THE NOVELS
       OF THOMAS HARDY, ed. Anne Smith (London: Vision
       Press, 1979) 107–25

       Familiar discussion of H's handling of Wessex folklore and
       superstition in *T*.

291   Elledge, Scott (ed.)
       THOMAS HARDY: *TESS OF THE D'URBERVILLES*:
       AN AUTHORITATIVE TEXT, HARDY AND THE
       NOVEL, CRITICISM, Norton Critical Editions (New
       York: Norton, 1965)

Usefully appends to the text more than twenty-five reviews, articles and extracts from criticism.

292   Freeman, Janet
       'Ways of Looking at Tess', *Studies in Philology* 79 (1982)
       311–23

Absorbing study of 'the way one looks – or fails to look' at Tess. H's ability to see her whole is 'the only imaginable good' in the novel's tragic world, yet even his way of viewing is shown to be 'yet another form of possession' which implicates him in the immorality he has deplored.

293   Gose, Elliot B.
       'Psychic Evolution: Darwin and Initiation in *Tess of the
       d'Urbervilles*', *Nineteenth-Century Fiction* 18:3 (December
       1963) 261–72

By tracing the novel's references to evolution and anthropology, especially primitive rituals, Gose seeks to show that Tess is not the victim of society but rather a victim caught in the 'ebb and flow of history, environment and self'.

294   Gregor, Ian
       'The Novel as Moral Protest: *Tess of the d'Urbervilles*',
       THE MORAL AND THE STORY by Ian Gregor and
       Brian Nicholas (London: Faber & Faber, 1962) 123–50.
       Extract in LaValley (306)

'For Hardy the story of Tess was the only story, it could accommodate within it everything he wanted to say, and in telling it he could reveal poverty, class privilege, cruelty, hypocrisy – it could be the substance of his moral protest.' Excellent and persuasive account of the novel's varying levels of imaginative intensity and their ultimate unity.

295   Grundy, Peter
       'Linguistics and Literary Criticism', *English* 30 (1981)
       151–69

Linguistic analysis of a passage from *T* (the final section of 'The Maiden').

296   Hazen, James
'Angel's Hellenism in *Tess of the d'Urbervilles*', *College Literature* 4 (Spring 1977) 129–35

Interesting thesis that H is much kinder to Angel Clare than most of the novel's critics, and the two men are shown to share many beliefs and ideas. H does not want to punish Angel; rather, his regression to a Christian outlook demonstrates the urgent need to reform such restrictive ethics.

297   Holloway, John
'*Tess of the d'Urbervilles* and *The Awkward Age*', THE CHARTED MIRROR: LITERARY AND CRITICAL ESSAYS (London: Routledge & Kegan Paul, 1960) 108–17

Henry James' novel, like *T*, documents 'a whole period of English life' and a whole society in its interaction with a 'distinctive human quality' (Innocence for James, the Pure Woman for H). Both novels develop an initial situation to a very extreme condition: in *T*, however, the stress is less on a moral one than on a 'human and emotional one'.

298   Horne, Lewis B.
'The Darkening Sun of Tess Durbeyfield', *Texas Studies in Literature and Language* 13 (1971–72) 299–311

A symbolic reading of the novel: the two major symbols are 'the sun and the land – the sun symbolizing the hope that is born, dies, and is born again, the land furnishing a kind of *paysage moralisé* against which the movement of hope and disillusionment takes place'.

299   Hugman, Bruce
HARDY: *TESS OF THE D'URBERVILLES* (London: Edward Arnold, 1970), Studies in English Literature Series

Slim volume, a useful introduction to the novel. Does not reflect the structure or sequence of *T*, but often offers interesting insights.

300   Jacobus, Mary
'Tess's Purity', *Essays in Criticism* 26 (1976) 318–38;

reprinted with alterations as 'Tess: The Making of a Pure
Woman', TEARING THE VEIL, ed. Susan Lipshitz
(London: Routledge & Kegan Paul, 1978) 77–92

Excellent scholarly account of H's changes in his conception
of Tess. The late, defiant addition of the sub-title is only one
of those 'lasting modifications' which H made in order to
argue a case for Tess 'whose terms were dictated by the
conventional moralists themselves'. To regard Tess as pure is
to see her as 'immune to the experience she undergoes',
depriving her of sexual autonomy, responsibility and tragic
status.

301   Johnson, Bruce
' "The Perfection of Species" and Hardy's Tess', NATURE
AND THE VICTORIAN IMAGINATION, ed. U. C.
Knoepflmacher and G. B. Tennyson (Berkeley: University
of California Press, 1977) 259–77

Excellent account of Darwin's influence on H, demonstrating
the novel's analogies between old landscapes, cultural sur-
vivals and family histories. Tess is the *ideal* pagan, and her
ancientness and the ideal quality of her consciousness are
expressed by geological and paleontological metaphors. She
may be a victim of modern society, but most importantly she
is a victim of 'Angel's denial of her true, truly Darwinian,
affinities with nature'.

302   Kelly, Mary Ann
'Hardy's Reading in Schopenhauer: *Tess of the
d'Urbervilles*', *Colby Library Quarterly* 18:3 (September
1982) 183–98

T contains H's 'darkest philosophical inclinations' because he
was 'assimilating Schopenhauer's godless and fatalistic philosophy' at the time of writing.

303   Kettle, Arnold
'*Tess of the d'Urbervilles*', in AN INTRODUCTION TO
THE ENGLISH NOVEL, Vol. 2, HENRY JAMES TO
THE PRESENT DAY (London: Hutchinson University
Library, 1953) 45–56

A well-written and provocative study, but its theme – that the tragedy of Tess is symbolic of the destruction of the English 'peasantry' by a parvenu ruling class figured in Alec d'Urberville – is pushed to an ideological extreme.

304   Laird, J. T.
'New Light on the Evolution of *Tess of the d'Urbervilles'*, *Review of English Studies* 31 (1980) 414–35

Supplements his book-length study (305), elaborating upon the later stages of the novel's composition and explaining the importance of two printed serial texts in relation to its main line of transmission.

305   Laird, J. T.
THE SHAPING OF *TESS OF THE D'URBERVILLES* (Oxford: The Clarendon Press, 1975)

Analyses evolution of *T* from manuscript through serial to novel in various editions. H increasingly defends Tess. Agricultural theme is increasingly prominent, as are the cosmic and the ancient family themes.

306   LaValley, Albert J. (ed.)
TWENTIETH CENTURY INTERPRETATIONS OF *TESS OF THE D'URBERVILLES* (Englewood Cliffs, N.J.: Prentice-Hall, 1969)

Editor's introduction surveys H's career and various aspects of *T*.

Part 1   Reprints extracts from Ian Gregor (294), Dorothy Van Ghent (319), Irving Howe (137), D. H. Lawrence (144), David Lodge (308), David J. De Laura (626). Also Arnold Kettle's 'Introduction' to *Tess* (New York: Harper & Row, 1966).

Part 2   Brief 'view points' discuss 'general Hardyean matters' relevant to *T*. Extracts from Douglas Brown (117) on the ballad, Irving Howe (137) on use of folk material, Benjamin Sankey on character portrayal, Ellen Moers on Tess as cultural stereotype, Albert Guerard on the originality of the novel, Edmund Blunden (113) on H's conversation about Tess, Douglas Brown (117) on social and individual fate in *T*. Concludes with relevant extracts from F. E. Hardy's *Life* (58).

Chronology of important dates, selected bibliography.

307 Lee, Vernon (Violet Page)
'The Handling of Words: T. Hardy', *English Review* 9 (September 1911) 231–41; reprinted in THE HANDLING OF WORDS AND OTHER STUDIES IN LITERARY PSYCHOLOGY (London: Lane; New York: Dodd, Mead, 1923) 222–41 (1968). Partly reprinted in Norman Page (ed.), THE LANGUAGE OF LITERATURE: A CASEBOOK (London: Macmillan, 1984) 176–81

Early and critical analysis of H's style, including a close reading of a passage from *T*. Finds H to be occasionally slovenly and undisciplined, although she adds that such imprecision may at times contribute to the depiction of lush and teeming life in the novel.

308 Lodge, David
'Tess, Nature, and the Voices of Hardy', LANGUAGE OF FICTION: ESSAYS IN CRITICISM AND VERBAL ANALYSIS OF THE ENGLISH NOVEL (London: Routledge & Kegan Paul; New York: Columbia University Press, 1966) 164–88. Pages 164–79 are reprinted in R. P. Draper (ed.), HARDY: THE TRAGIC NOVELS (90) 165–81. See also LaValley (306)

Distinguished stylistic account of *T*, showing how H 'is a peculiarly difficult novelist to assess because his vices are almost inextricably entangled with his virtues'. The breadth, variety and unexpectedness of his vision make enormous demands on his control of his verbal medium which he does not consistently achieve. One is 'tantalized by a sense of greatness not quite achieved'.

309 Miller, J. Hillis
'Fiction and Repetition: *Tess of the d'Urbervilles*', FORMS OF MODERN BRITISH FICTION, ed. Alan Warren Friedman (Austin and London: University of Texas Press, 1975) 43–71

T is 'structured around manifold repetitions – recurrences verbal, thematic and narrative. At the same time, it is a story about repetition.' The chains of connection or repetition that converge on a given passage (e.g. the scene of Tess's violation, which Miller discusses at length) are complex and diverse, and none has priority over the others. The reader can simply execute a lateral dance of interpretation without ever reaching 'a sovereign principle of explanation' about the novel.

310   Morton, Peter
        THE VITAL SCIENCE: BIOLOGY AND THE
        LITERARY IMAGINATION 1860–1900 (London: Allen &
        Unwin, 1984)

        Discusses H's response to contemporary controversies about heredity in *T*.

311   Paris, Bernard J.
        ' "A Confusion of Many Standards": Conflicting Value
        Systems in *Tess of the d'Urbervilles*', *Nineteenth-Century
        Fiction* 24:1 (June 1969) 57–79

        H's arguments in defence of Tess often contradict each other and do not produce any coherent moral vision. He cannot decide whether nature is moral or amoral, whether Tess is fallen or still 'innocent'. H seems willing to advance any argument to absolve Tess: 'Hardy is the biographer we all want'. The novel brilliantly renders Tess's sense of the world, but is inept at interpreting the meaning of her experience. Compare Schweik (313).

312   Rabiger, Michael
        'Tess and Saint Tryphena: Two Pure Women Faithfully
        Presented', THOMAS HARDY ANNUAL No. 3, ed.
        Norman Page (London: Macmillan, 1985) 54–73

        Seeks to show influence on *T* of a Breton mystery play about St Tryphena. Proceeds to discuss the role played by H's cousin, Tryphena Sparks, in the genesis of the novel. Occasionally plausible, sometimes ludicrous, essay.

313 Schweik, Robert C.
'Moral Perspective in *Tess of the d'Urbervilles*', *College English* 24 (October 1962) 14–18

Confident that the novel does possess some consistent understanding of Tess and her experience. The philosophical passages 'provide recognizably limited moral perspectives – partial insights into a much more complex moral reality revealed by the novel as a whole'. The stress here is on H's *conscious* use of such limited perspectives which, collectively, provide an overview of Tess. Schweik's argument is refuted by Bernard Paris (311).

314 Silverman, Kaja
'History, Figuration and Female Subjectivity in *Tess of the d'Urbervilles*', *Novel* 18:1 (1984) 5–28

Absorbing account of how the narrator's point of view '*constructs*' Tess, offering different subjective possibilities. At times Tess is allowed to melt into her background as a simple field woman, at others she is singled out from her fellow labourers and is out of place in her landscape. A deconstruction of Tess's sexuality leads to debatable conclusions, but the rape–seduction scene is afforded a very interesting reading.

315 Sommers, Jeffrey
'Hardy's Other *Bildungsroman: Tess of the d'Urbervilles*', *English Literature in Transition* 25 (1982) 159–68

Tess's passage from dream to reality is typical of the female 'novel of awakening', with its emphasis on false starts and reversals caused by her own temperament. By the end of the novel, Tess 'has matured, outgrowing the need for flight, sensing her destiny, accepting it'. Mythical and allegorical studies of *T* tend to ignore this detailed and realistic growth.

316 Tanner, Tony
'Colour and Movement in Hardy's *Tess of the d'Urbervilles*', *Critical Quarterly* 10 (Autumn 1968) 219–39; reprinted in R. P. Draper (ed.), HARDY: THE TRAGIC NOVELS (90) 182–208; and in Ian Watt (ed.) (108) 407–31

Poetic discussion of *T*, analysing significant images, especially the colour red, to show how H's impressionism depicts in Tess a type of human life drawn out from Nature but doomed to be destroyed by it. Many of the images, prominent as braille, act as visible omens of her destiny. Tanner is exhaustive in his pursuit of such images as blood, the sun, altars and tombs, walking and travelling.

317   Thompson, Charlotte
'Language and the Shape of Reality in *Tess of the d'Urbervilles*', *Journal of English Literary History* 50 (1983) 729–62

Absorbing, but occasionally turgid, study of 'the ruling principle' of the novel's universe, which is the power of the imaginative mind to influence, even alter, the material world. This can be achieved through language, which is both reactionary and innovative: it can preserve old, conventional mental structures, or it can reorganise and reform them through imaginative language. Metaphor and other rhetorical figures may reshape Tess's world and how we see it, but they can only rearrange the existing elements of that world, not create a new reality.

318   Tomlinson, T. B.
'Hardy's Universe: *Tess of the d'Urbervilles*', *Critical Review* 16 (1973) 19–38

Persuasive practical criticism demonstrates *T*'s combination of 'simplicity and sheer inventive individuality'. Sees H as endorsing in his greatest novel a philosophy of 'positive agnosticism'. There is no oppressive cosmic consciousness here to victimise man, and the suffering of Tess's life does not cancel out her infrequent happiness and understanding.

319   Van Ghent, Dorothy
'On *Tess of the d'Urbervilles*', THE ENGLISH NOVEL: FORM AND FUNCTION (New York: Holt, Rinehart & Winstan, 1953; reprinted New York: Harper, 1961) 195–209; reprinted in MODERN BRITISH FICTION; ESSAYS IN CRITICISM, ed. Mark Schorer (New York: Oxford University Press, 1961) 30–44; and in HARDY:

A COLLECTION OF CRITICAL ESSAYS, ed. Albert J.
Guerard (93) 77–90. See also LaValley (306)

Celebrated symbolic reading of *T:* 'it is Hardy's incorruptible
feeling for the actual that allows his symbolism its amazingly
blunt privileges and that at the same time subdues it to and
absorbs it into the concrete circumstance of experience, real
as touch.' Also defends the use of coincidence and accident:
'if the narrative is conducted largely by coincidence, the
broad folk background rationalizes coincidence by constant
recognition of the mysteriously "given" as what "was to be" –
the folk's humble presumption of order in a rule of mishap.'
Though the story is 'grounded deeply in a naturalistic
premise', the symbolism 'enforces a magical view of life'.

320   Waldoff, Leon
      'Psychological Determinism in *Tess of the d'Urbervilles',*
      CRITICAL APPROACHES TO THE FICTION OF
      THOMAS HARDY, ed. Dale Kramer (London:
      Macmillan, 1979) 135–54

A curiously old-fashioned approach to Tess, despite its
terminology. Begins by giving a survey of fate and other
forms of determinism (heredity, natural and social laws),
concluding that the degree of responsibility which Tess has
for her life is deliberately indeterminate and ambiguous (Was
it a rape? Was it a seduction?). Then proceeds to argue that
'the decisive determinant was all along an attitude held by
Angel' who, in Freudian terms, is unable to combine his
affectionate and sensual feelings – he cannot simultaneously
love and desire. The men may be victims of such a conflict,
but it is the woman who pays.

321   Wickens, G. Glen
      'Hardy and the Aesthetic Mythographers: The Myth of
      Demeter and Persephone in *Tess of the d'Urbervilles',*
      University of Toronto Quarterly 53 (1983–84) 85–106

Densely and often brilliantly argued thesis that the development of Tess's thoughts and feelings retraces 'the evolutionary "progress" of Western man from the age of myth' to
an age of critical and reflective thought. This collapse of
idealism 'hinders the spiritual evolution of [a society's] finest
individuals, like Tess'.

322   Wright, Terence
'Rhetorical and Lyrical Imagery in *Tess of the d'Urbervilles*',
Durham University Journal 24 (1972) 79–85

H is more interested in his novel's ' "poetic" form' than in
other structures such as plot. He achieves such form by the
use of symbolism, imagery and intense visual or emotional
scenes. Interesting comparisons with Henry James.

Jude the Obscure

323 Alvarez, Al
'Afterword', *JUDE THE OBSCURE* (New York: New American Library, 1961) 404–14; reprinted in Albert J. Guerard (ed.) (93) 113–22

Frustration is the permanent condition of Jude's life. Despite everything he can do, Sue remains a bodiless idea, an idea of something in himself. The essential subject of *JO*, however, is not Oxford, or marriage, or even frustration, but loneliness.

324 Basham, Diana
'*Jude the Obscure* and *Idylls of the King*', *Thomas Hardy Society Review* 1:10 (1984) 311–16

Convincing demonstration of the 'connection in Hardy's mind between his own novel, a story of failure and "unfulfilled aims", and the Laureate's [Tennyson's] own reconstruction of a more illustrious failure, that of the legendary Arthur in the *Idylls of the King*'. Basham indicates similarities of theme, intention and imagery.

325 Björk, Lennart A.
'Psychological Vision and Social Criticism in *Desperate Remedies* and *Jude the Obscure*' BUDMOUTH ESSAYS ON THOMAS HARDY [etc. – see 103] 86–105

Deals with influence of French utopian socialist Charles Fourier on H's psychological and social ideas.

326 Blake, Kathleen
'Sue Bridehead, "The Woman of the Feminist Movement"', *Studies in English Literature, 1500–1900* 18 (Autumn 1978) 703–26

Thorough, persuasive view of Sue as embodying divisions within Victorian feminism between asceticism and hedonism.

She is capable of love and 'gravitates' towards men who offer fulfilment, but she rejects their sexist view of her. Her attempt at liberation is 'daring and plausible', and H does not condemn her final conformity.

327   Bragg, Melvyn
'Thomas Hardy and *Jude the Obscure*', BUDMOUTH ESSAYS ON THOMAS HARDY [etc. – see 103] 106–24; reprinted in *Essays by Divers Hands: Being the Transactions of the Royal Society of Literature* 39 (1977) 24–46

Interesting discussion of H's *Literary Notebooks* and their relationship to *JO*, in which 'there was a most intense and painful collision of Hardy's past, his present, and his fiction'.

328   Buckley, Jerome Hamilton
'The Obscurity of *Jude*', SEASON OF YOUTH: THE BILDUNGSROMAN FROM DICKENS TO GOLDING (Cambridge, Mass.: Harvard University Press, 1974) 162–85

This chapter is part of Buckley's critical and historical survey of the Bildungsroman (he also discusses *David Copperfield, Great Expectations, The Mill on the Floss, Marius,* etc.). *JO* is seen as the first tragic Bildungsroman in English. A tactful account of H's autobiographical relationship with Jude. The conventions of the genre encourage H to 'objectify what he wishes to conceal, yet feels bound to express'. Jude manages to survive H's confusions, contradictions and his 'serious lapse in taste'.

329   Buitenhuis, Peter
'After the Slam of *A Doll's House* Door: Reverberations in the Work of James, Hardy, Ford and Wells', *Mosaic* 17:1 (Winter 1984) 83–96

A couple of pages on unhappy marriages in *JO*.

330   Burstein, Janet
'The Journey Beyond Myth in *Jude the Obscure*', *Texas Studies in Literature and Language* 15 (1973–74) 499–515

Exceptionally clear account of how H in *JO* 'rejected the notion of a fruitful return to a mythic way of knowing the experiential world and explored instead the problems of the human journey beyond myth', since 'the comfortably coherent world once conceived by the mythic mind' is now inaccessible.

331 Collins, Philip
'Pip the Obscure: *Great Expectations* and Hardy's *Jude*',
Critical Quarterly 19:4 (Winter 1977) 23–35

Pip and Jude are both working-class orphans whose social ambitions require a move from the country to the town. Numerous parallels indicated. H is frank where Dickens is morally circumspect.

332 Fass, Barbara
'Hardy and St Paul: Patterns of Conflict in *Jude the Obscure*', *Colby Library Quarterly* 10:5 (March 1974) 274–86

'It is not a question of whether Hardy's viewpoint in *Jude* is pagan or Christian. Like his own hero and Matthew Arnold, Hardy could see the necessity for the value of both, but he seems forced to assent to Heine's final belief that reconciliation is impossible,' a belief that echoes St Paul.

333 Fischler, Alexander
'An Affinity for Birds: Kindness in Hardy's *Jude the Obscure*', *Studies in the Novel* 13:3 (Fall 1981) 250–65

On H's use of the bird-bride verbal play in *JO*. Jude is fatally weak because he is kind to both.

334 Fischler, Alexander
'Gins and Spirits: The Letter's Edge in Hardy's *Jude the Obscure*', *Studies in the Novel* 16 (1984) 1–19

This innovating and amusing article examines H's pun in *JO* on 'gin' (the alcoholic version and the instrument of trapping), coupling this with 'spirits' of various kinds (Sue as a free spirit, Christminster's ghosts and Jude's drink). The brutality of entrapment in *JO* is brought out by the increasingly bitter ambiguities of the punning.

335   Gallivan, Patricia
'Science and Art in *Jude the Obscure*', NOVELS OF
THOMAS HARDY, ed. Anne Smith (London: Vision
Press, 1979) 126–44

Fascinating study of H's reading in contemporary psychology (especially the work of Henry Maudsley) and how it influenced his presentation in *JO* of hallucinations, perceptual disorders, delusions and the inheritance of neurotic tendencies. Jude and Sue undergo opposing intellectual developments: Jude moves through what Maudsley called a 'process of progressive disillusioning', while Sue retreats into guilt, fear and orthodoxy, 'a reversion to the old belief of savages'. Convincing argument that 'the most vividly imaged passages' of *JO* can be seen as 'passages of pure psychological realism'.

336   Giordano, Frank R. Jr
'*Jude the Obscure* and the Bildungsroman' *Studies in the Novel,* Thomas Hardy Special Number 4:4 (Winter 1972) 580–91

Jude's final rejection of society is so absolute that it makes the novel virtually a satire of the Bildungsroman. Compare Buckley (328).

337   Goetz, William R.
'The Felicity and Infelicity of Marriage in *Jude the Obscure*', *Nineteenth-Century Fiction* 38:2 (1983) 189–213

Social custom is seen in *JO* as a form of natural law, not as an alternative to it; Sue's return to Phillotson thus seems inevitable. Similarly, marriage and divorce are not opposed, both being equally unstable conditions. This is a sophisticated investigation of the marriage question as one involving the nature of language and the status of the 'letter' of the law.

338   Goode, John
'Sue Bridehead and the New Woman', WOMEN WRITING

AND WRITING ABOUT WOMEN, ed. Mary Jacobus
(London: Croom Helm; New York: Barnes & Noble, 1979)
100–13

Feminist reading of *JO*, defending Sue as an 'exposing image'
whose 'incomprehensibility' constitutes the novel's effect.
Sue is above all an image, the object of male understanding;
she is so destructive because she utters herself, whereas, in
the ideology of sexism, she ought to be an image to be
uttered.

339   Gregor, Ian
        'Jude the Obscure', IMAGINED WORLDS: ESSAYS ON
        SOME ENGLISH NOVELS AND NOVELISTS IN
        HONOUR OF JOHN BUTT, ed. Maynard Mack and Ian
        Gregor (London: Methuen, 1968) 237–56

Excellent reading of *JO*, stressing 'how dominantly it is
concerned with an internal quest for the reality of the self'.
The Wessex landscape disappears, because in *JO* 'the conflict
is interiorized, one temperament with another, so that place
becomes a matter of little significance, the essential landscape is of heart and nerves'. If *JO* may seem to be a
miscellany of subjects, this is because H recognised the
'multiple ways' in which his theme could be regarded; he
refused totality and inclusiveness of vision, accepting instead
'disjunctions'.

340   Hassett, Michael E.
        'Compromised Romanticism in *Jude the Obscure'*,
        Nineteenth-Century Fiction 25:4 (March 1971) 432–43

Jude settles for limited, concrete, embodiments of his ideals.
He and Sue do not transform reality but merely create
imaginative substitutes for it, and the novel thus questions
the practical value of Romanticism.

341   Heilman, Robert B.
        'Hardy's Sue Bridehead', *Nineteenth-Century Fiction*, 20
        (March 1966) 307–23; reprinted in R. P. Draper (ed.),
        HARDY: THE TRAGIC NOVELS (90) 209–26

Sue is a psychological study of coquettishness, professing unconventional opinions but dangerously unaware that she is, at the level of emotional response, fundamentally conservative. By a curiously relevant emotional logic, she punishes herself by returning to the most rigid extreme of conventionality. This is a profoundly typical theme in H's novels, seen here as an instance of that 'habitual rational analysis that tends to destroy the forms of feeling developed by the historical community'. Heilman's study is a model of close reading for a particular purpose, but his conclusion that Sue's fate is more an 'illness' than a tragedy suggests that concentration on the psychology of a single character may distort the effect of the novel as an artistic whole.

342   Heilman, Robert B.
'Introduction', *Jude the Obscure,* ed. Robert B. Heilman (New York: Harper and Row, 1966) 1–46

Judicious, balanced analysis of *JO,* stressing H's use of irony, contrasts and 'social complaint'. The characters are not allegorical figures in the satiric structure, for they are allowed to develop spontaneously, and Sue, especially, is a 'work of genius' who steals the novel from Jude.

343   Holland, Norman
'*Jude the Obscure*: Hardy's Symbolic Indictment of Christianity', *Nineteenth-Century Fiction* 9:1 (June 1954) 50–60

Thorough analysis of *JO*'s Christian symbolism, which H employs to criticise late Victorian Christian society and, especially, the ideal of self-sacrifice.

344   Hoopes, Kathleen R.
'Illusion and Reality in *Jude the Obscure*', *Nineteenth-Century Fiction* 12:2 (September 1957) 154–7

Brief but concise account of the gap between Jude's dreams and experiences.

345   Horne, Lewis B.
'Pattern and Contrast in *Jude the Obscure*', *Etudes Anglaises* 32:2 (1979) 143–53

Structural contrasts underline the disparity between hope and actuality. Two of *JO*'s major controlling symbols, the journey and the cell, are ambivalent (e.g. the cell can be seen as refuge or prison). The novel's six parts are patterned concentrically; for example, the first section, with its boyish dreams of Christminster, is balanced by the final section which shows Jude's despair. Similarly, parts 2 and 5 show the expectation and the reality of marriage respectively.

346   Howe, Irving (ed.)
       'Introduction', *JUDE THE OBSCURE,* Riverside edition
       (Boston: Houghton Mifflin, 1965)

Vigorous defence of *JO*'s modernity, with its emphasis on doubt and crisis, pain and deracination. The traditional and the modern exist in 'a kind of sustaining friction' with each other, and the central characters live in that 'amorphous and ill-charted arena in which irrational impulses conflict with one another'. Howe converts what have often been described as defects of the novel (its incoherence and indeterminacy) into virtues.

347   Ingham, Patricia
       'The Evolution of *Jude the Obscure*', *Review of English Studies* 27 (1976) 27–37, 159–69

Scrupulous and thorough account of *JO*'s textual history, showing H's alterations and stressing the importance of the manuscript. Ingham disagrees with Paterson (357) in his belief that H began with the university theme and only later moved on to attack the marriage laws. She believes instead that H was from the outset concerned with the question of marriage, 'and that in dealing with marriage he was engrossed by the nature of the human relationship', rather than with the stringency of the laws.

348   Jacobus, Mary
       'Sue the Obscure', *Essays in Criticism* 25 (1975) 304–29

Excellent defence of H's portrayal of Sue, whose tragedy complements and illuminates Jude's. She may appear highly individual and 'obscure' but it is precisely this 'realistic sense of the gap between what she thinks and what she does, between belief and behaviour' which 'imparts unique complexity and life to the static contrasts of the novel's original conception'. H's intention in *JO* may be incompletely realised, 'but the novel is not less suggestive, and its protest not less eloquent, for that'.

349   Knoepflmacher, U. C.
'The End of Compromise: *Jude the Obscure* and *The Way of All Flesh*', LAUGHTER & DESPAIR: READINGS IN TEN NOVELS OF THE VICTORIAN ERA (Berkeley, Los Angeles and London: University of California Press, 1971) (1973)

H's uncompromising stance makes *JO* 'an elegy lamenting the death of nineteenth-century idealism'. It is not a novel of social protest, for Jude is rather the victim of his creator's 'dim view of an existence drained of all hope'. The novel is not a tragedy, but it succeeds nevertheless because 'the cosmic cruelty [H] feels so intensely permeates the novel from beginning to end'. (Especially interesting discussions of Father Time, Arabella and the pig-sticking scene.)

350   Langland, Elizabeth
'A Perspective of One's Own: Thomas Hardy and the Elusive Sue Bridehead', *Studies in the Novel* 12:1 (Spring 1980) 12–28

Absorbing account of how Sue escapes from the limited point of view from which the narrator and Jude view her: 'the grinder of analysis is an inadequate tool for capturing Sue's character'. Persuasive discussion of H's bias against her.

351   Leavis, L. R.
'The Late Nineteenth Century Novel and the Change Towards the Sexual – Gissing, Hardy and Lawrence', *English Studies* 66 (1985) 36–47

Highly readable and denigrating view of H as a literary vulgariser, especially in *JO*, which fails as a feminist or a social novel. H is merely sensationalising the work of George Eliot and Gissing, blatantly relying on coincidence. Sue Bridehead is a 'curious amalgam' of the feminist and the unemancipated, and it took D. H. Lawrence (144) to make

JO 'a more coherent novel than the one Hardy actually wrote'. Polemical and very stimulating iconoclasm.

352 Lodge, David
'*Jude the Obscure*: Pessimism and Fictional Form',
CRITICAL APPROACHES TO THE FICTION OF
THOMAS HARDY, ed. Dale Kramer (London:
Macmillan, 1979) 193–201; reprinted in Lodge's WORKING
WITH STRUCTURALISM: ESSAYS AND REVIEWS
ON NINETEENTH- AND TWENTIETH-CENTURY
LITERATURE (London: Routledge & Kegan Paul, 1981)
106–13

Describes the series of parallels and recurrences in *JO* which demonstrate that 'life is a closed system of disappointment from which only death offers an escape'. A sound but unremarkable thesis.

353 McDowell, Frederick P. W.
'Hardy's "Seemings or Personal Impressions"': The Symbolic Use of Image and Contrast in *Jude the Obscure*', *Modern Fiction Studies* 6 (Autumn 1960) 233–50

This essay is firmly in the 'symbolic' school of H criticism and gives a thorough (though occasionally insistent) discussion of images (musical, Biblical, animalistic, etc.) in *JO*. The novel becomes a kaleidoscope with multiple perspectives and 'changing vistas of meaning'. McDowell gives a necessary corrective to the reductive naturalistic interpretations of *JO*, but he does not say whether all these patterns of imagery ever converge or come into clear focus.

354 McDowell, Frederick P. W.
'In Defense of Arabella: A Note on *Jude the Obscure*', *English Language Notes* 1:4 (June 1964) 274–80

The animal imagery connected with Arabella belittles and imbalances her stature. She is frank, shrewd and large-natured, a credible antagonist to Jude. H no doubt intended his 'lusty Arabella' to produce 'a shudder among his genteel readers'. Critics who condemn her are responding to the allegorical implications of the novel, rather than to H's realistic portrayal of her. (Refreshing, if rather chivalrous, character sketch.)

355   Mizener, Arthur
       '*Jude the Obscure* as a Tragedy', *Southern Review* 6
       (Summer 1940) 193–213

       JO is not tragic or symbolic, but is in fact a naturalistic
       chronicle showing the 'history of a worthy man's education'.
       It cannot be a tragedy since the obstacles to Jude's education
       are not permanent or universal and the novel does not
       contrast 'the permanently squalid real life of man with the
       ideal life', as a tragedy ought to do. In the absence of such
       tragic tension, Jude's life and death are meaningless. This
       autobiographical reading of *JO* rests on questionable assump-
       tions about tragedy but is provocative and lively.

356   Newey, Vincent
       '*Jude the Obscure*: Hardy and the Forms of Making',
       Proceedings of the English Association North 1 (1985) 29–52

       Using modern critical practices, Newey explores the reader's
       engagement in the 'making' of *JO*, a novel which 'draws
       attention to modes of textuality'.

357   Paterson, John
       'The Genesis of *Jude the Obscure*', *Studies in Philology* 57
       (1960) 87–98

       Analyses the 'basic reorganisation in conception' which the
       manuscript of *JO* reveals. The original conception of the
       story was strikingly at variance with the finished novel: 'what
       was undertaken as a critical examination of the educational
       system in Hardy's time came inadvertently, in its working
       out, to take in an equally critical examination of the
       sacrament and institution of marriage.' (Yet compare Ingram
       (347).)

358   Pinion, F. B.
       '*Jude the Obscure*: Origins in Life and Literature',
       THOMAS HARDY ANNUAL No. 4, ed. Norman Page
       (London: Macmillan, 1986) 148–64

       Circumspect reflections on autobiographical incidents in *JO*.
       Also suggests various literary influences (Shelley, Carlyle,

Tennyson and Sarah Grand's novel, *The Heavenly Twins,* published in 1893).

359   Rachman, Shalom
'Character and Theme in Hardy's *Jude the Obscure',* *English* 22 (Summer 1973) 45–53

Analyses some themes in *JO* (such as nature, marriage, time and education) to show that 'the characters are created through the themes and in a sense they are the themes'. The two most important themes are flesh and spirit.

360   Saldívar, Ramón
'*Jude the Obscure*: Reading and the Spirit of the Law', *Journal of English Literary History* 50 (1983) 607–25

It is crucial that the basic conflicts of the novel occur in the context of marriage, since civil law attempts to codify the rules for social intercourse. Jude opposes a *literal* reading of these rules, yet his *figural* one leads to no spiritual truth. 'On the contrary, Jude's illusions result from a figurative language taken literally, as with Sue he takes "Nature at her word".' A fascinating study of Jude's attempt to 'read' and translate his world, and his repeated illusion of a single readable truth.

361   Slack, Robert C.
'The Text of Hardy's *Jude the Obscure',* *Nineteenth-Century Fiction* 11:4 (March 1957) 261–75

Excellent detailed study of H's alterations to *JO* in its various editions, such as his more sympathetic view of Sue and his wish to make the pizzle-throwing episode less explicit.

362   Sondstroem, David
'Order and Disorder in *Jude the Obscure',* *English Literature in Transition* 24:1 (1981) 6–15

Describes, with the help of a diagram, the complexity of Jude's career.

363   Sumner, Rosemary
'Hardy as Innovator: Sue Bridehead', *Thomas Hardy
Society Review* 1:5 (1979) 151–4

H's portrayal of Sue's sexual neuroses was his most striking
innovation, but H does not give a clinical analysis, stressing
that she is ultimately 'unstateable'.

364   Van Tassel, Daniel E.
'"Gin-drunk" and "Creed-drunk": Intoxication and
Inspiration in *Jude the Obscure*', *Thomas Hardy Society
Review* 1:7 (1981) 218–21

Detailed analysis of *JO*'s references to wine, gin, religion and
inspiration, concluding that Sundays are very bad days for
Jude.

365   Williams, Merryn
'Hardy and "the Woman Question"', THOMAS HARDY
ANNUAL No. 1, ed. Norman Page (London: Macmillan,
1982) 44–59

Very informed contextual study of Sue Bridehead and the
New Woman, showing how contemporary novelists such as
Gissing, Grant Allen and Olive Schreiner had depicted
questions of marriage, divorce and employment for women.
Concludes that H, while sympathetic to improving the status
of women, created no tough New Women in his fiction since
'women, for him, remained victims, because they had been
born "the Weaker"'.

366   Wright, Janet B.
'Hardy and his Contemporaries: The Literary Context of
Jude the Obscure', *Inscape* 14 (1980) 135–50

Describes H's familiarity with novels about the New Woman
in the early 1890s.

The Minor Novels

General studies

367 Gatrell, Simon
'Middling Hardy', THOMAS HARDY ANNUAL No. 4,
ed. Norman Page (London: Macmillan, 1986) 70–90

Examines H's writing between 1879 and 1884, especially *TM*
and *TT* ('middling Hardy novels') to show that H could
'achieve fine work beyond the bounds of Wessex tragedy'.
Stresses H's attempts here 'to discover to what extent
buildings can embody the essentials of his human story in the
way that the Heath does' in *RN*.

368 Hochstadt, Pearl R.
'Hardy's Romantic Diptych: A Reading of *A Laodicean* and
Two on a Tower', *English Literature in Transition* 26:1
(1983) 23–34

L and *TT* are both 'love stories pure and simple', showing
that H was 'as ready to imagine a comic as a tragic
presentation of romantic love', and that he was willing to
assign such love 'an unequivocally positive value'. Interesting
comparison of these two novels' presentation of love with
that of *T*.

369 Morrell, Roy
'Some Aspects of Hardy's Minor Novels', BUDMOUTH
ESSAYS ON THOMAS HARDY [etc. – see 103] 60–73

TM is difficult to take seriously, unlike *PBE*, H's most
'deeply felt' book till *MC*. In *HE*, such coherence as the
book possesses comes from Ethelberta herself. *TT* has been
seriously underrated, and it has a *well*-contrived plot. *WB*
deserves more attention, and even *L* has its good moments.

370 Taylor, Richard H.
THE NEGLECTED HARDY: THOMAS HARDY'S
LESSER NOVELS (London: Macmillan, 1982)

A very welcome and successful attempt to rehabilitate critical interest in H's minor works. While not seeking to propose a radical reappraisal of the comparative rankings of H's novels, Taylor nevertheless sees it as mistaken 'to isolate the lesser novels as separate and distinct, as aberrations and failures', since they each play an essential part in the 'dynamic process' of H's development as a writer. To exclude them from critical consideration is to 'distort his career and to disguise the interpenetrating unities of his fiction'. Seven chapters give individual attention to *DR, PBE, HE, TM, L, TT* and *WB*.

Desperate Remedies

371   Beatty, C. J. P.
'*Desperate Remedies* 1871', THOMAS HARDY YEAR BOOK, No. 2 (1971) 29–38

Enthusiastic discussion of how *DR* and later novels show evidence of H's training as an architect. Many references to H's obsession with framing devices, sight lines, measurement, spatial configurations and, above all, shape. This is an excellent and important contribution to our understanding of H's use of perspective and architectural practices.

372   Johnson, Trevor
'*Desperate Remedies*: A Hardy Palimpsest', *Thomas Hardy Journal* 1:1 (January 1985) 32–40

Ingeniously suggests that H interpolated into *DR* a long blank verse speech, simply setting it out as prose to obscure the line divisions. H's 'dry jest' at the expense of publishers who rejected his poetry is said to appear in Chapter 13:4 ('Though it may be right . . . I seem to them to be').

373   Jones, Lawrence O.
'*Desperate Remedies* and the Victorian Sensation Novel', *Nineteenth-Century Fiction* 20:1 (June 1965) 35–50

DR shows conflict between H's '"idiosyncratic mode of regard"' and the conventions demanded by a late Victorian audience. The potentially tragic love story gives way to melodrama and suspense. Initially, the characters are more complex than the sensation novel requires and seem to promise a study of irrational sexuality, but they eventually become mere stereotypes.

374 Moore, Kevin Z.
'The Poet within the Architect's Ring: *Desperate Remedies, Hardy's Hybrid Detective-Gothic Narrative'*, *Studies in the Novel* 14:1 (Spring 1982) 31–42

DR is 'a tale about life's tragic ironies which is told on two levels, the rational and the imaginative'. The romantic dilemma of reconciling science and religion, reason and emotion, is reflected in the narrator's precarious position: 'his interest is Gothic; his narrative procedures are, in the main, those of the detective novel'. He thus gives rational explanations while retailing irrational events.

375 Ousby, Ian
'Class in *Desperate Remedies*', *Durham University Journal* 76:2 (1984) 217–22

The sensation novel usually shows an uncritical admiration of land, property and gentry, but H's effort in the genre takes the side of the socially inferior. The tensions in the narrative are a product of H's inability to repress his social criticism.

376 Page, Norman
'Visual Techniques in Hardy's *Desperate Remedies*', *Ariel* 4:1 (January 1973) 65–71

Demonstrates how H, in his first published novel, uses those modes of vision (spying, framing, etc.) which were to become 'a permanent and prominent feature of his technique'.

377 Ward, Paul
'*Desperate Remedies* and the Victorian Thriller', THOMAS HARDY YEAR BOOK No. 4 (1974) 72–6

H *intended DR* to be a derivative thriller, with Miss Aldclyffe's secret as its central interest, but the fate of Cytherea Graye is the real centre of the novel, since H could not subordinate his concern with his characters' emotional

predicaments to the exigencies of the thriller plot. Some
interesting comparisons are made with Wilkie Collins; in
spite of himself, H wrote a more distinctive novel than he
planned.

378   Wickens, G. Glen
'Romantic Myth and Victorian Nature in *Desperate
Remedies*', *English Studies in Canada* 8:2 (June 1982)
154–73

DR has some principles of composition that deserve more
praise than the novel is usually given, such as its large
controlling image, 'the contrast between two gardens, a
cultivated nature and a wilderness'. In *DR*, H is asking 'when
should nature be cultivated or spontaneity embraced' and is
seeking 'to mediate between the Victorian extremes of the
scientific and the sacramental ideas of nature'.

379   Wittenberg, Judith Bryant
'Thomas Hardy's First Novel: Women and the Quest for
Autonomy', *Colby Library Quarterly* 18:1 (March 1982)
47–54

H's 'much vaunted sympathy for women is covertly undermined by narrative developments'. Miss Aldclyffe in *DR* is
'punished' for being latently lesbian. Even the portrayal of
Tess is undermined by H's 'manipulative', even faintly
sadistic, narrative stance.

A Pair of Blue Eyes

380   Amos, Arthur K.
'Accident and Fate: The Possibility for Action in *A Pair of
Blue Eyes*', *English Literature in Transition* 15:2 (1972)
158–67

PBE is not as pessimistic as it might seem, for it postulates
'more rewarding possibilities than those realized in the
surface story'. The possibility of self-assertion is not ruled
out.

381   Miller, J. Hillis
THE FORM OF VICTORIAN FICTION (Notre Dame and
London: University of Notre Dame Press, 1968) passim

Studies a passage from Chapter 27 of *PBE* to demonstrate
how temporal perspectives determine form and meaning in
Victorian fiction. 'Many different related temporal rhythms'
coexist, such as those of the reader, the author, the narrator
and the characters, and each expresses 'a present which lives
and moves in the yearnings of its incompletions'. A densely
argued piece anticipating Miller's book on H (147).

382   Steig, Michael
'The Problem of Literary Value in Two Early Hardy
Novels', *Texas Studies in Literature and Language* 12
(Spring 1970) 55–62

Pursues the novel argument that *PBE* is superior to *FMC*, in
that 'it offers no reassurance to reconcile us to the claims of
the super-ego, of society and convention'. This contrasts with
H's evasion and 'moralistic management' of fantasy in *FMC*,
where the emphasis is on repression, discipline and consequent reward.

The Hand of Ethelberta

383   Gittings, Robert
'Findon and *The Hand of Ethelberta*', *Thomas Hardy
Society Review* 1:10 (1984) 306–7

Traces source of ghastly scene in *HE*, in which Ethelberta
and Picotee come across a knacker's yard. Gittings explains
that H, in his twenties, used to visit a girl in Findon, where
such a yard existed. The gruesome episode has a basis in
reality.

384   Schwarz, John H.
'Misrepresentations, Mistakes, and Uncertainties in *The
Hand of Ethelberta*', *Thomas Hardy Journal* 1:2 (May 1985)
53–62

Illustrates *HE*'s skilful use of misleading behaviour (inten-
tional or otherwise) and mistaken or uncertain perceptions

'to echo and reinforce and modify his story line of the struggling woman whose worldly success depends largely on her ability to deceive'.

385   Short, Clarice
'In Defense of *Ethelberta*', *Nineteenth-Century Fiction* 13:1 (June 1958) 48–57

Useful survey of previous views of *HE*. Describes (rather than defends) H's conception of comedy here, with its absence of gods and its cool, but not uncaring, heroine. Ethelberta's social triumph is the reward of her intellect.

386   Ward, Paul
'*The Hand of Ethelberta*', THOMAS HARDY YEAR BOOK No. 2 (1971) 38–45

HE offers 'a fascinating commentary on the relationship between the tragic and comic masks'. *HE* has many of the themes of H's tragic novels, but they are shown in a comic perspective by his reductive attention to '*inessential* details' which deflate the potential for tragedy. This is a positive and detailed analysis of the novel, especially good on H's narrative distance.

387   Wing, George
'"Forbear, Hostler, Forbear!": Social Satire in *The Hand of Ethelberta*', *Studies in the Novel* 4:4 (Winter 1972) 568–79

On *HE*'s occasional comic and satiric successes.

The Trumpet-Major

388   Johnson, H. A. T.
'In Defence of *The Trumpet-Major*', BUDMOUTH ESSAYS ON THOMAS HARDY [etc. – see 103] 39–59

Useful survey of previous dismissive criticism of the novel. Suggests influence of the Augustan novel. It lacks a unifying principle present in all of H's major novels but it has a 'poetic integrity'. Good on H's use of the Mill and the Camp.

389 Rignall, J. M.
'The Historical Double: *Waverley, Sylvia's Lovers, The Trumpet-Major*', *Essays in Criticism* 34:1 (1984) 14–32

Excellent account of *TM* and H's successful 'creation of a comic world on a black ground, the fleeting rescue of life from the oblivion of recorded history'. The fictional world of the historical novel is circumscribed by a darkness which, as we move through the nineteenth-century, 'becomes an increasingly potent presence, anticipating the epistemological uncertainty and historical scepticism of the modern novel'. Fissures may threaten to develop in the narrative, such as when the Trumpet-Major walks out of fictional Wessex into the bloody reality of the Peninsula Wars.

A Laodicean

390 Drake, Robert Y.
'*A Laodicean*: A Note on a Minor Novel', *Philological Quarterly* 40 (1961) 602–6

H appears to have 'rigged' the conflict in *L*, which is not, as we are led to expect, a struggle between traditional and modern (such a fruitful one in his major novels) but one between 'an emasculated traditionalism and a fairly compassionate modernism'. The novel is nevertheless an illuminating commentary on 'those divisions within the human heart' which H depicted more forcefully elsewhere.

391 Jarrett, David W.
'Hawthorne and Hardy as Modern Romancers',
Nineteenth-Century Fiction 28:4 (March 1974) 458–71

Principally discusses influences of *The House of the Seven Gables* on *L*. Both authors wish to revitalise romance conventions and bring them 'into the world of Victorian scientific, social, and philosophic "progress"'. *L* combines the Gothic house and ancestral portraits with an interest in photography and railways. H's use of romantic elements here tends towards 'clarification and simplification, even at the expense of subtlety'.

392   Larkin, Peter
'Absences and Presences: Narrative Bifurcation in *A Laodicean*', *Thomas Hardy Society Review* 1:3 (1977) 81–6

Discusses how 'potential relationships between characters are actualised or modified through the device of one figure "spying" on another'. Detailed analysis of two chapters. The novel shows that H's instinct for 'striking structural narrative solutions was alive and well'.

393   Pettit, Charles P. C.
'A Reassessment of *A Laodicean*', *Thomas Hardy Society Review* 1:9 (1983) 276–82

The first 100 pages of *L* are 'a superb example of Hardy at his best', rich, expansive and assured, with real characters and setting. Also, 'nowhere else outside *Jude the Obscure* do intellectual ideas play such a major part in a Hardy novel'. H became ill during the writing of *L*, and the rest of the book becomes a thriller, whose faults Pettit describes with much gusto.

394   Wing, George
'Middle-class Outcasts in Hardy's *A Laodicean*', *Humanities Association Review* 27:3 (1976) 229–38

Concentrates on Dare and de Stancy as introducing a note of 'malignancy' and sadness to the romantic comedy in their 'aberration from middle-class Victorian acceptances'.

Two on a Tower

395   Bayley, John
'The Love Story in *Two on a Tower*', THOMAS HARDY ANNUAL No. 1, ed. Norman Page (London: Macmillan, 1982) 60–70

A welcome, positive and often excellent analysis of *TT*, focusing especially on the various manifestations of Lady Constantine, who appears, in the hut at the base of the great tower, as captive maiden, maternal Venus and married woman cooking breakfast. H's conception of her is more subtle and effortless than his portrayal of Eustacia Vye, who resembles her in a bolder but cruder manner.

396   Ebbatson, J. R.
'Thomas Hardy and Lady Chatterley', *Ariel* 8:2 (April 1977) 85–95

Suggests that *TT* was an influence on D. H. Lawrence's novel.

397   Sumner, Rosemary
'The Experimental and the Absurd in *Two on a Tower*', THOMAS HARDY ANNUAL No. 1, ed. Norman Page (London: Macmillan, 1982) 71–81

Provocative revaluation of *TT*. While not denying its minor status, Sumner argues that the use of the stellar universe as background to the action makes it a daring and experimental novel. The indifferent cosmos which the telescope reveals has resemblances to the void, abyss and absurd world of Conrad, Forster and Beckett. Excessive plotting however swamps H's interesting but not wholly successful experiment with the Absurd, although the farcical complications of the action have their own function in this absurd world.

398   Wing, George
'Hardy's Star-Cross'd Lovers in *Two on a Tower*', THOMAS HARDY YEAR BOOK 14 (1987) 35–44

The conflict in the novel stems from the fact that 'Swithin's immature emotions are in contrast to his precocious intellect whereas Viviette's intellectual indifference is in contrast to her sexual longings of a frustrated and older woman'. His arrested development ensures that 'it is her love, rather than Swithin's, which forms the greater magnitude'.

The Well-Beloved

399   Fowles, John
'Hardy and the Hag', THOMAS HARDY AFTER FIFTY YEARS, ed. Lance St John Butler (London: Macmillan, 1977) 28–42

Provocative study of *WB*, examining its psychosexual origins in H's imagination. The novel, 'seething as it is with the suppressed rage of the self-duped', was written to assuage his 'private guilt' and 'self-disgust' at his own 'morbid and narcissistic imagination'.

400   Gerber, Helmut E.
'Hardy's *The Well-Beloved* as a Comment on the Well-Despised', *English Language Notes* 1:1 (September 1963) 48–53

Sees *WB* as H's bitter valediction to novel writing. The contrast between the idealistic Pierston and the compromising Somers reflects H's bitterness at having to sacrifice his own artistic integrity to public tastes. *WB* is 'a far less feeble curtain speech' than has usually been thought. (Occasionally rather fanciful, but takes *WB* seriously as a sketch of the artistic temperament.)

401   Priestley, Alma
'Hardy's *The Well-Beloved*: A Study in Failure (with some reference to Proust's success)', *Thomas Hardy Society Review* 1:2 (1976) 50–9

Discusses Proust's admiration for *WB*, especially its portrayal of subjective love. Shows autobiographical basis to the character of Jocelyn.

402   Ryan, Michael
'One Name of Many Shapes: *The Well-Beloved*', CRITICAL APPROACHES TO THE FICTION OF THOMAS HARDY, ed. Dale Kramer (London: Macmillan, 1979) 172–92

Excellent analysis of H's bitter and ironic final novel, a 'mock fable which makes fun of both the Platonic aestheticism of the latter part of the century and the innocuous, popular society novel which Hardy's publishers would have preferred he write'.

403 Wing, George
'Theme and Fancy in Hardy's *The Well-Beloved*', *Dalhousie Review* 56:4 (Winter 1976–77) 630–44

As a tragi-comedy, *WB* suffers not so much from frivolity but much more from the 'noises of mechanical stress'. A direct and often scathing analysis of *WB*, noting its occasional comic successes.

Shorter Fiction

404   Bates, H. E.
THE MODERN SHORT STORY: A CRITICAL
SURVEY (Boston: The Writer, 1941) 37–43, 81–2, 169, 217

H's short stories are 'choked crudely to death' by his Latinate
style and tendency towards moralising; he is like a man
'trying to paint a picture with a dictionary'. A vivid criticism
of H, but little analysis of the short stories.

405   Beachcroft, T. O.
THE MODEST ART: A SURVEY OF THE SHORT
STORY IN ENGLISH (London: Oxford University Press,
1968) passim

Like D. H. Lawrence, H seems uninterested in the formal
properties of the short story. At his best, though, H is 'a poet
of the story', as in 'The Trampwoman's Tragedy'.

406   Benazon, Michael
'Dark and Fair: Character Contrast in Hardy's "Fiddler of
the Reels"', *Ariel: A Review of International English
Literature* 9:2 (April 1978) 75–82

A rather schematic set of oppositions is drawn between Mop
and Ned, who represent the rural and the urban, the old and
the new, the lover and the husband. Such a contrast of
characters is similar to that in *MC* between Henchard and
Farfrae. Mop Ollamoor ('all *amour*') is a romantic archetype
offering sexual fulfilment, but Car'line chooses the security of
Ned instead.

407   Benazon, Michael
'"The Romantic Adventures of a Milkmaid": Hardy's
Modern Romance', *English Studies in Canada* 5:1 (1979)
56–65

Benazon regards this tale as one of the more successful of H's short fictions, with its keen psychological analysis of female behaviour and its neo-Shakespearean world of fantasy and romance.

408   Brady, Kristin
THE SHORT STORIES OF THOMAS HARDY (London: Macmillan; New York: St Martin's Press, 1982)

The first book devoted to H's stories. A very welcome and successful revaluation of them, stressing the coherence and unity of each volume and emphasising H's formal innovations and manipulation of narrative perspective, which at times seem distinctly modernist. Principally discusses *Wessex Tales, A Group of Noble Dames* and *Life's Little Ironies*. Final chapter on *A Changed Man* and other stories.

409   Carpenter, Richard C.
'How to Read *A Few Crusted Characters'*, CRITICAL APPROACHES TO THE FICTION OF THOMAS HARDY, ed. Dale Kramer (London: Macmillan, 1979) 155–71

A welcome and eloquent plea not to neglect H's minor works. Adopts a 'reader response' approach to examine 'how the work *moves* as the reader encounters it, what *happens* in the process of reading'.

410   Fischler, Alexander
'Theatrical Techniques in Thomas Hardy's Short Stories', *Studies in Short Fiction* 3 (Summer 1966) 435–45

H likes to produce dramatic tableaux and to manipulate or 'direct' characters to indicate their lack of free will. A valuable insight into H's use of narrative distance and perspective.

411   Gatrell, Simon
'The Early Stages of Hardy's Fiction', THOMAS HARDY ANNUAL No. 2, ed. Norman Page (London: Macmillan, 1984) 3–29

Detailed textual study of H's working practices, showing how he would progress from source-notes to plot outlines, then to half-developed sketches, draft manuscripts and fair-copy manuscript. Most of the discussion concerns the genesis and evolution of some short stories, especially 'A Few Crusted Characters'.

412   Giordano, Frank R.
'Characterization and Conflict in Hardy's "The Fiddler of the Reels"', *Texas Studies in Literature and Language* 17 (1975–76) 617–33

This story shows H's moral ambiguity and narrative irresolution. It has an allusive mode of characterisation, a 'mythopoeic exhibition of Wessex "history"' and a representation of irreconcilable conflicts, the central one being the 'clash of Hebraic and Pagan Greek values'.

413   Haarder, A.
'Fatalism and Symbolism in Hardy: An Analysis of "The Grave by the Handpost"', *Orbis Litterarum* 34:3 (1979) 227–37

A reply to critics of H's pessimism. The tale uses Christian symbolism to express H's longing for a lost faith, coupled with his awareness of its extinction.

414   Keys, Romey T.
'Hardy's Uncanny Narrative: A Reading of "The Withered Arm"', *Texas Studies in Literature and Language* 27:1 (Spring 1985) 106–23

This story is a striking example of H's 'manipulations of narrative form and theme'. It cannot easily be classified as a supernatural tale, since 'an interpretive knot woven of narrative gaps, recurrences, and shifting levels of reality bedevils the reader'. Indeed, H intended here to subvert the supernatural tale, producing a collision of forms which urge us to read it as 'an essay in the pathology of sexual jealousy, a story built around coincidence, and/or a psychological fable'.

415 O'Connor, William Van
'Cosmic Irony in Hardy's "The Three Strangers"', *English Journal* 47 (May 1958) 248–54, 262

The story is not successful, since there is no necessary connection between the action and the tale's meaning, but it does exhibit H's ironic perspective in the conflict between man's desire for happiness and his wish to make restrictive laws.

416 Page, Norman
'Hardy's Short Stories: A Reconsideration', *Studies in Short Fiction* 11 (Winter 1974) 75–84

Refuses to dismiss the stories as pot-boilers, and argues that they have three areas of interest: they show the range of his writing, they have significant relationships with the novels and they illustrate in miniature 'some of the complex problems of composition and revision' typical of H's work. Especially interesting account of revisions to 'On the Western Circuit'. Four groupings of stories: the humorous; the romantic or supernatural; the realistic, ironic or tragic and finally, the historical. Page concentrates on the second and third of these groups. [Reprinted in slightly different form in Page (152).]

417 Quinn, Maire A.
'Thomas Hardy and the Short Story', BUDMOUTH ESSAYS ON THOMAS HARDY [etc. – see 103] 74–85

H's art in the short stories 'is concerned not with the isolated incident but with the connected series'. Good on H's use of narrators, oral tales and the 'creation of a story-telling ambience'.

418 Roberts, James L.
'Legend and Symbol in Hardy's "The Three Strangers"', *Nineteenth-Century Fiction* 17:2 (September 1962) 191–4

There is no cosmic irony in the story. The use of legend and Christian symbolism stresses the innate importance of human beings.

419   Smith, J. B.
       'Dialect in Hardy's Short Stories', THOMAS HARDY
       ANNUAL No. 3, ed. Norman Page (London: Macmillan,
       1985) 79–92

       Thorough and detailed account, principally describing dialect
       as indicative of social class. A linguistic rather than literary
       appreciation of the stories.

420   Wain, John (ed.)
       'Introduction', SELECTED STORIES OF THOMAS
       HARDY (London: Macmillan, 1966) ix–xx

       Placing H's stories in the tradition of the country tale, Wain
       in his introduction argues that H has 'no respect for the short
       story as a literary form'. The stories are therefore 'more
       satisfying in their incidental qualities than in their overall
       impression', although H does excel as 'a writer of superb,
       evocative documentary'.

421   Wilson, Keith
       'Hardy and the Hangman: The Dramatic Appeal of "The
       Three Strangers"', *English Literature in Transition* 24:3
       (1981) 155–60

       Praise for H's dramatic skill in 'The Three Wayfarers', an
       adaptation of his short story.

422   Wing, George
       '*A Group of Noble Dames*: "Statuesque dynasties of
       delightful Wessex"', THOMAS HARDY ANNUAL No. 5,
       ed. Norman Page (London: Macmillan, 1987) 75–101

       A welcome, very detailed and largely thematic analysis of
       this volume of short stories, with their 'disarming simplicity'.

Poetry

Book-length studies

423   *Agenda* 10: 2–3 (Spring–Summer 1972)

Thomas Hardy Special Number. Distinguished collection of
original articles on the poetry by John Peck (516, 517), F.R.
Southerington (715), Thom Gunn (487), C.H. Sisson (532),
D. Drew Cox (473), David Wright (543), Richard Swigg
(535), Robert Pinsky (519), William H. Pritchard (523),
Henry Gifford (482) and Donald Davie (474). Also contains
poems on H, translations of poems, and Eugenio Montale's
'A Note on Hardy the Poet'.

424   Bailey, J. O.
THE POETRY OF THOMAS HARDY: A HANDBOOK
AND COMMENTARY (Chapel Hill, N.C.: University of
North Carolina Press, 1970)

Each poem is discussed separately, identifying characters,
places and ideas, and includes relevant facts of publication
and revision. Includes notes on H's *Collected Poems,* previously unpublished or uncollected poems, *D,* and *The Queen
of Cornwall.* Extensive bibliography. This work, and Pinion's
companion (433), are the two principal handbooks on H.

425   Buckler, William E.
THE POETRY OF THOMAS HARDY: A STUDY IN
ART AND IDEAS (New York: New York University
Press, 1983)

Buckler begins by examining the *Life,* which he finds to be a
paradigm of H's central artistic principle-cum-method, con-
sisting as it does of discontinuous impressionism, rather than
authenticated narrative. He then examines the poems as
similar evidence of that transformation of 'the autobio-

graphical tradition' by 'converting it from confession to drama'. Many perceptive close readings, stressing that each poem is *a* voice rather than *the* voice; often shrewd distinctions are made between what is said by the poem's persona and what emerges from the more carefully detached artefact through which he speaks.

426   Clements, Patricia and Grindle, Juliet (eds)
       THE POETRY OF THOMAS HARDY (London: Vision Press, 1980)

       Collection of eleven new essays, each aiming to regard the poems both 'as poetry and not another thing' and as products of their time and place. Essays annotated individually: see Isobel Grundy (486), Ronald Marken (506), S. C. Neuman (509), Rosemary L. Eakins (478), Jeremy V. Steele (534), Cornelia Cook (472), G. Glen Wickens (559), Patricia Ingham (494), Patricia Clements (470), Simon Gatrell (480) and Jon Stallworthy (533).

427   Davie, Donald
       THOMAS HARDY AND BRITISH POETRY (New York: Oxford University Press, 1972; London: Routledge & Kegan Paul, 1973)

       A contentious, exciting book which begins from the proposition that H has been 'the most far-reaching influence, for good and ill' on British poetry of the last fifty years. Features of such poetry as 'an apparent meanness of spirit, a painful modesty of intention, extremely limited objectives' fall into place if they are seen as an inheritance from H. For H, the poet should be one who is thoroughly acquainted with a region, but who is under no obligation to understand international politics. Davie's chapter on 'Hardy as Technician' gives welcome attention to H's craftsmanship.

428   Gibson, James
       THOMAS HARDY: THE MAKING OF POETRY (London: Macmillan, 1971)

       Audiovisual teaching package, with pamphlet, record and illustrations. Shows how H's poetry 'grows out of life'.

429   Gibson, James and Johnson, Trevor (eds)   ·
THOMAS HARDY: *POEMS:* A CASEBOOK (London:
Macmillan, 1979)

Excellent introduction surveys H's reputation as a poet.

> Part One: Extracts from H's *Personal Notebooks* (21), *The
> Life* (58), Letters and prefaces.
> Part Two: Critical Comment up to 1928. Sixteen reviews
> and early appreciation by such critics as Edward
> Thomas, Lytton Strachey, J. Middleton Murry
> and I. A. Richards.
> Part Three: Critical Comment Since 1928. Sixteen articles or
> extracts from books by Arthur S. MacDowall,
> F. L. Lucas, Howard Baker (462), C. Day Lewis
> (501), Douglas Brown (117), Samuel Hynes
> (430), C. B. Cox and A. E. Dyson (442),
> L.E.W. Smith, Philip Larkin, Kenneth Marsden
> (431), Jean Brooks (116), Thom Gunn (487),
> David Cecil (469), T. R. M. Creighton (8),
> William W. Morgan (508) and Frank R.
> Giordano (444).

430   Hynes, Samuel
THE PATTERN OF HARDY'S POETRY (Chapel Hill,
N.C.: University of North Carolina Press; London: Oxford
University Press, 1961). Excerpts in Gibson and Johnson
(eds), A CASEBOOK (429) 168–79, and in Albert J.
Guerard (ed.) (93) 161–74

The principal pattern is that H 'saw experience as a con-
figuration of opposites, every event contradicted or qualified
by a succeeding event, an infinite sequence of destructive
tensions'. Since these tensions are never reconciled or
synthesised, his work is antinomial rather than dialectical,
and it is this 'antinomial tension between his thought and his
feelings that gives his verse its characteristic pattern and its
integrity, and which gives order, though a minimal order, to
the chaos of experience'.

Hynes's book is very readable, although he feels obliged to
make the customary admissions of H's weaknesses (he saves
poems like other men save string). Yet 'there remains a core
of fine poetry', for 'fidelity to Life' is 'at the heart of Hardy's
greatness'.

431   Marsden, Kenneth
       THE POEMS OF THOMAS HARDY: A CRITICAL
       INTRODUCTION (London: Athlone; New York: Oxford
       University Press, 1969)

       Urbane and enthusiastic study, not seeking to beat any
       particular drum. Particularly impressive is Marsden's careful
       analysis of H's vocabulary, which is reprinted in Gibson and
       Johnson (eds), A CASEBOOK (429) 191-201.

432   Paulin, Tom
       THOMAS HARDY: THE POETRY OF PERCEPTION
       (London: Macmillan, 1975)

       Much of H's work shows his positivism and sceptical empiri-
       cism, but his imagination was not 'wholly governed by a
       despotic eye' and he refused to be 'the absolute prisoner of
       his sense impressions', achieving at times a visionary freedom
       and contradicting his own pessimism. Paulin offers numerous
       close readings of poems, and H's aesthetic of perception is a
       useful principle of organisation here, rather than a thesis
       doggedly pursued. Arguably the best book-length study of
       the poetry.

433   Pinion, F.B.
       A COMMENTARY ON THE POEMS OF THOMAS
       HARDY (London: Macmillan, 1976; New York: Harper &
       Row, 1977)

       Valuable handbook, similar in coverage to Bailey (424).
       Discusses each volume of poems, gives notes on most
       individual poems. Glosses dialect words, archaisms, neo-
       logisms, allusions. Cross-references to novels, letters, etc.
       Biographical background.

434   Richardson, James
       THOMAS HARDY: THE POETRY OF NECESSITY
       (Chicago and London: University of Chicago Press, 1977)

       Stimulating four chapters on H's poetry, examining especially
       his views on necessity and possibility, and his affinities with
       Browning.

435   Southworth, James Granville
       THE POETRY OF THOMAS HARDY (New York:
       Columbia University Press, 1947; revised 1966)

       Notable in being the first critical book devoted entirely to the
       poetry. It is difficult to see why Southworth bothered, since
       he is so lukewarm and unsympathetic.

436   Taylor, Dennis
       HARDY'S POETRY, 1860–1928 (London: Macmillan,
       1981)

       Thorough attempt to discern a pattern in H's poetry, whose
       central concern is 'what happens to an experience as it is
       made into literature, the experience remembered, the litera-
       ture reread' in a recurring cycle. This pattern is closely
       related to what Taylor regards as H's principal achievement,
       the 'meditative lyric'; as H 'meditates about the world, the
       world changes around him and intrudes on the meditation'.
       Taylor's attempt to find the thread in H's poetry is sometimes
       schematic and procrustean, especially in its insistence on H's
       'development' as a poet, but it is nevertheless a continually
       rewarding and innovative book. The final section offers an
       especially intensive study of H's war poetry.

437   *Victorian Poetry* 17:1–2 (Spring–Summer 1979)

       Special double number commemorating the fiftieth anni-
       versary of H's death.
          Ten articles (all but one original) by the following authors,
       annotated separately: I. A. Richards (527), Trevor Johnson
       (495), Richard Benvenuto (465), Peter Simpson (455), Ian
       Ousby (512), Kathryn R. King and William W. Morgan
       (498), Frank R. Giordano, Jr (484), William E. Buckler
       (440), Harold Orel (556) and Keith Wilson (560).
          Also includes 'Illustrations for *Wessex Poems*' and a
       number of original poems about H. A substantial and
       handsome tribute to H.

438   Zietlow, Paul
       MOMENTS OF VISION: THE POETRY OF THOMAS
       HARDY (Cambridge, Mass.: Harvard University Press,
       1974)

An outstanding study of H's poetry, presenting a comprehensive view (omitting *D*), and stressing 'the diversity and complexity of Hardy's achievement'. Most of the chapters review the poems according to type: poems of ironic circumstance, ballads and narratives, philosophical fantasies, poems of the personal and historical past, love poems and 'moments of vision' or brief poems of the present moment. The general progression of the book is from 'poems in which Hardy establishes a distance between himself and his subjects, to those in which he makes a direct, personal revelation'.

Studies of individual poems and 'Poems of 1912–13'

439   Bevan, Mary
       'Time's Derision and the Poems of 1912–1913', *Thomas Hardy Society Review* 1:10 (1984) 323–6

       Brief analyses of certain poems show H trying to 'transcend, even abolish, time, and assert the present reality of the past'. In these elegiac poems, H 'enacts a new love affair with the vision of Emma reclaimed from the past'. Competent account of a familiar interpretation.

440   Buckler, William E.
       'The Dark Space Illumined: A Reading of Hardy's "Poems of 1912–13" ', *Victorian Poetry* 17: 1–2 (Spring–Summer 1979) 98-107; reprinted in Buckler (574) 297–309

       Poetry itself is a prime theme of the elegies, for poetic expression is the chief hope for spiritual renewal, enabling him to probe and reconcile warring memories. The poems are monitored by a mythic subtext (principally the myth of Orpheus and Eurydice) which gives H an imaginative strategy by which he can 'conceive of his private responses generically'.

441   Casagrande, Peter J.
       'The Fourteenth Line of "In Tenebris, II" ', THOMAS HARDY ANNUAL No. 2, ed. Norman Page (London: Macmillan, 1984) 110-30

Argues that this line ('Who holds that if way to the Better there be, it exacts a full look at the Worst') does not support H's 'evolutionary meliorism'; rather, it deserves to be read 'as a lament for a lost paradise associated with the innocence of childhood' whose irrecoverable loss is precisely the Worst which must be faced. Interesting comments on the insistent and disabling nostalgia as seen in *T, JO* and *WB*.

442   Cox, C. B., and Dyson, A. E.
MODERN POETRY: STUDIES IN PRACTICAL CRITICISM (London: Edward Arnold, 1963) 33–40; reprinted in Gibson and Johnson (eds), A CASEBOOK (429) 180–5

Valuable demonstration of close reading techniques applied to 'After a Journey'.

443   Coxon, Peter W.
'Thomas Hardy: "The Voice" and Horace: Odes II, xiv', *Thomas Hardy Society Review* 1:9 (1983) 291–3

H uses metrical pattern of a Horace ode ('Eheu fugaces') in 'The Voice'.

444   Giordano, Frank R., Jr
'Hardy's Farewell to Fiction: The Structure of "Wessex Heights"', THOMAS HARDY YEAR BOOK no. 5 (1975; published 1976) 58–66. Partly reprinted in Gibson and Johnson (eds), A CASEBOOK (429) 253–63

Positive reading of the poem whose central theme is 'the speaker's quest for imaginative freedom'. It is not about a guilty and unloving traitor; rather, it shows 'a lonely writer who would liberate himself from the painful memories of obtuse critics and from the inhibiting preoccupation with his past fictional creations, in order to create in a newer and higher form of art, poetry'.

445   Hazen, James
'The God-Curst Sun: Love in "Neutral Tones"', *Victorian Poetry* 9 (1971) 331–8

Stimulating close reading of H's poem, showing the complex image of the sun as a symbol of love. 'Neutral Tones' is so successful because 'it uses natural images so effectively to sketch in psychological states and to relate them to a convincing human drama'.

446   Hillyard, Nicholas
'The Draft of "Retty's Phases"', *Thomas Hardy Society Review* 1:8 (1982) 257–62

Textual examination of the earliest manuscript of a poem by H to survive.

447   Leavis, F. R.
'Reality and Sincerity: Notes in the Analysis of Poetry', *Scrutiny* 19 (Winter 1952–53) 90–8; reprinted in THE LIVING PRINCIPLE: 'ENGLISH' AS A DISCIPLINE OF THOUGHT (London: Chatto & Windus, 1975) 127–54

Excellent practical critique of 'After a Journey'.

448   Mason, H. A.
'Wounded Surgeons', *Cambridge Quarterly* 11 (1982) 219–23

Interesting discussion of 'The Self-Unseeing'; where Leavis praised its particularity, Mason stresses instead that its greatness lies in its general truth.

449   May, Charles E.
'Hardy's "Darkling Thrush": The "Nightingale" Grown Old', *Victorian Poetry* 11 (1973) 62–5

Demonstrates parallels between H's poem and Keats' 'Ode to a Nightingale'. Suggests that H purposely inverted Keats' romantic view of nature and saw his bird's ecstatic song as ironic amidst its bleak surroundings.

450   Miller, J. Hillis
'Thomas Hardy, Jacques Derrida, and the "Dislocation of Souls"', TAKING CHANCES: DERRIDA, PSYCHOANALYSIS, AND LITERATURE, ed. Joseph

H. Smith and William Kerrigan (Baltimore and London: Johns Hopkins University Press, 1984) 135–45

A study of H's poem, 'The Torn Letter', with reflections on the ability of writing to create phantom recipients of letters.

451   Miller, J. Hillis
' "Wessex Heights": The Persistence of the Past in Hardy's Poetry', *Critical Quarterly* 10 (1968) 339–59

A thorough, close reading of this poem, stanza by stanza, with occasional glances at other novels and poems by H. The central theme of the poem, and of all H's work, is 'the impossibility of freeing oneself wholly from the past'.
    Reprinted and slightly augmented as 'History as Repetition in Thomas Hardy's Poetry: The Example of "Wessex Heights"', in VICTORIAN POETRY, Stratford-upon-Avon Studies 15, ed. Malcolm Bradbury and David Palmer (London: Edward Arnold, 1972) 222–53.

452   Morgan, William W.
'Form, Tradition, and Consolation in Hardy's "Poems of 1912–13"', *PMLA* 89 (May 1974) 496–505

Urges us to read 'Poems of 1912–13' as an organized whole, rather than as twenty-one separate poems. The volume has a five-part linear structure, 'a movement from *recent past* to *present*, then from *distant past* to *recent past* to *present*'. The passage through pain to consolation is gradual and difficult. Excellent at showing both the 'firm traditional ties' and the 'bold originality' of H's elegy for his deceased wife. Since Morgan's classifications of the temporal sequence are occasionally too clear-cut, this is a provocative stimulus for tutorial discussion.

453   Murfin, Ross C.
'Moments of Vision: Hardy's *Poems of 1912–13*', *Victorian Poetry* 20:1 (1982) 73-84

The woman whose death these poems lament was not the real Emma but her 'imagined, phantasmal counterpart' whose invention permits H to gain consolation 'through the making of grief: good times and precious people are created and then much missed'. A sensitive and subtle reading of the poems, especially good on the links between H's evasive strategies here and those in his other volumes of poetry.

454   Ousby, Ian
' "The Convergence of the Twain": Hardy's Alteration of Plato's Parable', *Modern Language Review* 77 (1982) 780–96

In this poem and in his novels (especially *JO*), H draws on Plato's account of Aristophanes' myth that men and women are divided parts of an original whole trying, often tragically, to reunite.

455   Simpson, Peter
'Hardy's "The Self-Unseeing" and the Romantic Problem of Consciousness', *Victorian Poetry* 17:1–2 (Spring–Summer 1979) 45–50

Close reading of H's poem which Simpson views as 'an exploration of the paradox of self-consciousness'. The poem is ambiguous about consciousness: the dream necessarily excludes a sense of reality, but reality offers nothing that is preferable to the dream and is therefore a 'privileged condition'.

456   Weatherby, H. L.
'Of Water and the Spirit: Hardy's "The Voice" ', *Southern Review* 19 (1983) 302-9

Comprehensive analysis of the poem, showing how its allusions to the Greek New Testament may contradict the apparent despair.

Articles and chapters in books: general themes in Hardy's poetry

457   Alexander, Michael
'Hardy Among the Poets', THOMAS HARDY AFTER FIFTY YEARS, ed. Lance St John Butler (London: Macmillan, 1977) 49–63

Excellent account of the modern and traditional aspects of H's poetry, stressing the 'tributary influences' of Browning and Wordsworth. H's poetry, like the latter's, 'moves from observation and description to a more generally symbolic presentation', and Alexander gives successful analyses of 'After a Journey', 'Under the Waterfall' and 'Afterwards' to support his case.

458 Arkans, Norman
'Hardy's Narrative Muse and the Ballad Connection',
THOMAS HARDY ANNUAL No. 2, ed. Norman Page
(London: Macmillan, 1984) 131–56

Excellent account of H's relation to the traditional and literary ballad, showing how H's narrative poems are part of that nineteenth-century development of the ballad in which 'speakers gained prominence, telling became self-fulfilling, and the reader was soon entangled in the conflict between the so-called impersonality of the ballad and the personality of the speaking voice, the one having a story to tell, the other having to tell a story'. Gives close readings of 'The Rash Bride', 'Burning the Holly' and, especially, 'The Bride-Night Fire'.

459 Arkans, Norman
'Hardy's Poetic Landscapes', *Colby Library Quarterly* 15:1
(March 1979) 19–35

Wide-ranging and often acute essay on H's ' "idiosyncratic mode of regard" ' in his poetry which stresses that 'a way of perceiving reality leads to a meaningful engagement of it'.

460 Auden, W. H.
'A Literary Transference', *Southern Review,* Thomas Hardy
Centennial Edition, 6 (Summer 1940) 78–86; reprinted in
Albert J. Guerard (ed.) (93) 135–42

A loving tribute to the power and skill of H's poetry, beautifully expressed. 'What I valued most in Hardy, then, as I still do, was his hawk's vision, his way of looking at life from a very great height.'

461   Bailey, J. O.
'Evolutionary Meliorism in the Poetry of Thomas Hardy',
Studies in Philology 60 (July 1963) 569–87

Traces H's growing optimism that 'human action can make
the circumstances of life and life itself better in ethical quality
and in happiness'. The process of the 'wakening of the Will'
culminates in *D*.

462   Baker, Howard
'Hardy's Poetic Certitude', *Southern Review,* Thomas Hardy
Centennial Edition 6 (Summer 1940) 49–63; partly reprinted
in Gibson and Johnson (eds), A CASEBOOK (429) 137–46

Forthright declaration of H's 'staunch humanity' in his
poetry, where he 'shakes himself free from familiar half-
truths and settles himself upon his own hard truth'. Even the
most pessimistic utterances of his verse, when they are
properly motivated, lead to a 'chastening of the spirit' akin to
that of religious literature. 'More than any other poet he
found substance for poems in the everyday histories of simple
people.'

463   Barzun, Jacques
'Truth and Poetry in Thomas Hardy', *Southern Review,*
Thomas Hardy Centennial Edition 6 (Summer 1940) 179–92

Persuasive treatment of ideological aspects of the verse,
arguing that H reminds us constantly that he treats truth
poetically. He was pragmatic in his Romanticism, knowing
that 'Truth and Poetry do not fight a manichean fight which
will leave Science or Ignorance master of the field: they
merge into each other by degrees and constitute together the
sum total of mind-measured reality.' Barzun shows the value
of bringing the poems to bear on the fiction.

464   Bayley, John
'Separation and Non-Communication as Features of Hardy's
Poetry', *Agenda* 14 (Autumn 1976) 45–52

Analyses those poems by H in which that 'kind of consciousness which goes with the power to communicate, with
one-self or others, has come retrospectively, or too late'.

Poems discussed include 'The Self-Unseeing' and 'The Darkling Thrush'.

465   Benvenuto, Richard
'The Small Free Space in Hardy's Poetry', *Victorian Poetry* 17:1–2 (Spring–Summer 1979) 31–44

Possibilities of freedom and choice do exist in H's verse. Freedom for H's characters is not a matter of breaking through the prison walls, for there is nothing outside the prison. However, they are free to determine how to react to prison life and 'free to give their lives a moral substance by breaking the law' within jail. From the cosmic view, the universe appears as a giant prison, but this perspective is opposed by a 'personalized vision' and it is in those moments of freedom which this 'specific awareness of living things' grants that moral action takes place.

466   Blackmur, R. P.
'The Shorter Poems of Thomas Hardy', *Southern Review,* Thomas Hardy Centennial Edition 6 (Summer 1940) 20–48; reprinted in LANGUAGE AS GESTURE (New York: Harcourt, Brace, 1952) 51–79

A generally depreciating survey of H's verse. H is said to break with tradition in favour of his 'adherence to his personal and crotchety obsessions', and he is the 'great example of a sensibility violated by ideas'. Blackmur wants to weed out of the canon H's poems about ideas, since he is rarely successful except on those occasions when his 'personal rhythm' finds a 'liberating subject' (usually death or the dead). H succeeds in 'The Workbox', 'Last Words to a Dumb Friend' and a couple of dozen other poems.

467   Buckler, William E.
'Victorian Modernism: The Arnold–Hardy Succession', *Browning Institute Studies* 11 (1983) 9–21

Similarities between the poems of Arnold and H include the uses of the dramatic monologue and the contemporary mood of the 'darkling plain'. Interesting comparison of 'Dover Beach' and 'Wessex Heights'.

468   Carpenter, Richard
'Hardy's Dramatic Narrative Poems', *English Literature in Transition* 9:4 (1966) 185–6

Ten per cent of H's poems have the pattern and length of the 'dramatic narrative', with its emphasis on plot and conflict, reminiscent of the traditional ballad.

469   Cecil, Lord David
'The Hardy Mood', THOMAS HARDY AND THE MODERN WORLD (104) 106–12; reprinted, with a small omission, in Gibson and Johnson (eds), A CASEBOOK (429) 232–8

Elegant celebration of the qualities of H's poetry, which reveals H to be 'exquisitely appreciative of delicate shades of feeling and of fleeting nuances of beauty'.

470   Clements, Patricia
' "Unlawful Beauty": Order and Things in Hardy's Poems', THE POETRY OF THOMAS HARDY, ed. Patricia Clements and Juliet Grindle (London: Vision Press, 1980) 137–54

Fascinating account of H's 'constant re-shaping of sense', concentrating especially on those many poems of return which 'present moments in which experience expands, so that the mind must in response either open or close, re-draw its design of the world or confirm its isolation in its formalization of what it has seen before'. In such moments of re-vision, H 'isolates the mind in an experience of shock, of thrilling perception, and he forces it to reorganize or retreat'.

471   Collins, Michael J.
'Comic Technique in the Poems of Thomas Hardy', THOMAS HARDY YEAR BOOK 11 (1984) 31–6

The device of reversal of expectations can produce comedy as well as sadness in H's poems. Analyses chiefly 'Ah, Are You Digging on My Grave?', 'The Ruined Maid', 'The Contretemps' and 'Channel Firing'.

472 Cook, Cornelia
'Thomas Hardy and George Meredith', THE POETRY OF
THOMAS HARDY, ed. Patricia Clements and Juliet
Grindle (London: Vision Press, 1980) 83–100

Able treatment of the two poets who share 'similarly
"modern" subjects or ways of seeing'.

473 Cox, D. Drew
'The Poet and the Architect', *Agenda* 10:2–3 (1972) 50–65

Examines H's career as an architect and draws analogies
between his architectural interests and the form of his verse:
he has the ability to combine 'technological' and 'Gothic'
skills, craftsmanship and ornamentation.

474 Davie, Donald
'Hardy's Virgilian Purples', *Agenda* 10:2–3 (Spring–Summer
1972) 138–56

Celebrated attempt to end the notion of H as a 'sturdily
simple soul'. Beginning with an account of Virgil's influence
on H's poetry, Davie proceeds to show how H 'was a
remarkably devious and tortuous man – just the sort of man
who would at once convey and cloak his meanings with the
allusive deviousness that I have been trying to demonstrate'.
Remarkably affirmative reading of 'Poems of 1912–13'.

475 Dollimore, Jonathan
'The Poetry of Hardy and Edward Thomas', *Critical
Quarterly* 17:3 (Autumn 1975) 203–15

The best of H's poems possess 'a kind of integrity of
awareness', honest in spite of vulnerability. He is one of
those poets whose lesser verse is a corollary of their best, for
his weaker poems lack that precarious balance between
honesty and vulnerability and settle instead for an 'assumed
pessimism – an attitude decided on before, or as a substitute
for, experience'. In contrast to Edward Thomas, 'for Hardy
there is usually something tangible in the external world, and
in inanimate nature especially, that focuses feeling'. Many
points of difference between the two authors: an excellent
account of their respective strengths.

476   Draper, Ronald Philip
       'Hardy: Illusion and Reality', LYRIC TRAGEDY (London:
       Macmillan, 1985) 111–30

       Draper examines a number of H's lyrics to show how his
       sense of tragedy depends on his acute feeling for the
       interaction of romantic illusion and a more realistically based
       disillusionment. Poems given detailed comment include:
       'Proud Songsters', 'The Bullfinches', 'Winter in Durnover
       Field', 'Neutral Tones', 'Beyond the Last Lamp', 'At Castle
       Boterel', 'The Going', 'After a Journey', 'During Wind and
       Rain', and 'The Convergence of the Twain'. H's most
       movingly tragic lyrics come from the combination of 'intimate
       domestic detail' and 'controlled, but not quite mastered,
       personal grief and guilt'.

477   Draper, Ronald Philip
       'Hardy's Love Poetry', MULTIPLE WORLDS,
       MULTIPLE WORDS: ESSAYS IN HONOUR OF IRENE
       SIMON, ed. H. Maes-Jelinek, P. Michel and P.
       Michel-Michot (Liège: University of Liège, 1988) 79–96

       Draper examines the romantic and anti-romantic strains in
       H's love poetry, and pays special attention to the sympathy
       with the woman's point of view which is characteristic of
       many of the poems written after the death of Emma: 'H
       delved into his own memory to re-discover what it was like to
       be once (forty years ago) passionately in love, and into the
       imagined mind of Emma to find what it was like to be other
       than himself.'

478   Eakins, Rosemary L.
       'The Mellstock Quire and Tess in Hardy's Poetry', THE
       POETRY OF THOMAS HARDY, ed. Patricia Clements
       and Juliet Grindle (London: Vision Press, 1980) 52–68

       Discusses how characters, incidents and themes in *UGT* and
       T are also the subject of a number of poems. To re-read the
       fiction in the context of such poems is to be 'impressed anew
       by the energy of the novels' more diffused life'.

479   Fletcher, Pauline
       'Rossetti, Hardy, and the "hour which might have been"',
       Victorian Poetry 20:3–4 (1982) 1–13

Outlines 'tantalizing links and parallels' between the poems of H and D.G. Rossetti, who is said to resemble the poet Trewe in 'An Imaginative Woman'.

480   Gatrell, Simon
'Travelling Man', THE POETRY OF THOMAS HARDY, ed. Patricia Clements and Juliet Grindle (London: Vision Press, 1980) 155–71

On the many uses of the journey motif in H's poetry, such as walking, pilgrimages and chance encounters on a road. Journeying permits contact with nature and provides a ready metaphor for life.

481   Gibson, James
'The Poetic Text', THOMAS HARDY AND THE MODERN WORLD (104) 113–27

Fascinating textual study of editions of H's poetry, ending with a plea for all of his work to be properly edited.

482   Gifford, Henry
'Hardy's Revisions *(Satires of Circumstance)*', *Agenda* 10:2–3 (Spring–Summer 1972) 126–37

Discusses the changes which H made to poems in *Satires of Circumstance* when preparing his *Collected Poems*. Especially interesting on revisions to 'Poems of 1912–13'.

483   Giordano, Frank R., Jr
'Hardy's Moments of Revision', BUDMOUTH ESSAYS ON THOMAS HARDY [etc. – see 103] 168–79

H's 'moments of revision' are poems which originate 'as a response to, or a comment upon, an earlier work or works of literature', deliberately artificial and allusive. Giordano examines certain works in *Wessex Poems* which respond to Wordsworth, Shelley, Tennyson, Browning and Arnold.

484   Giordano, Frank R., Jr
'A Reading of Hardy's "A Set of Country Songs"',
Victorian Poetry 17:1–2 (Spring–Summer 1979) 85–97

These eighteen poems show H's 'complex understanding and celebration of the "eternal verities" of country life'. Not since Wordsworth have the country folk been rendered so articulate. H's country songs permit one to hear 'intermittent sounds of joy and laughter amid the still, sad music of humanity'.

485   Gittings, Robert
       'The Improving Hand: The New Wessex edition of the *Complete Poems'*, THOMAS HARDY AFTER FIFTY YEARS, ed. Lance St John Butler (London: Macmillan, 1977) 43–8

Appreciative review of James Gibson's edition, focusing on poems with biographical interest.

486   Grundy, Isobel
       'Hardy's Harshness', THE POETRY OF THOMAS HARDY, ed. Patricia Clements and Juliet Grindle (London: Vision Press, 1980) 1–17

Exceptionally readable defence of H's 'harshness' such as his use of 'very new, very old, and very unusual words, periphrasis, inversion, oddities of syntax, imagery and sound' which all arise out of his 'experimental and inventive approach to language in general'. Such a style serves to make us 'wonder at the usual' and is 'perfectly fitted to convey a sense of the anomalous position, in his view, of consciousness in a universe of nescient striving forces'.

487   Gunn, Thom
       'Hardy and the Ballads', *Agenda* 10:2–3 (1972) 19–46; partly reprinted in Gibson and Johnson (eds), A CASEBOOK (429) 217–32

Much of H's poetry is in ballad form, 'but even in those that are not literally ballads, some or all of the ballad-characteristics are likely to be present. The diction tends to be plain and colloquial, the grotesque and the supernatural are present as a matter of course, and above all the structure of the narrative is economical, with incident and explanation implied wherever possible.' Engaging and very accessible essay.

488 Harvey, Geoffrey
'Thomas Hardy's Poetry of Transcendence', *Ariel*, 9:4
(1978) 3–20

Excellent close readings of that small group of H's visionary
poems which exhibit the 'transcending freedom' of memory,
love or the sense of place. In these vital poems, H 'strives to
establish an authentic mode of being predicated on existence
itself and on his own capacity to transcend it'. Paradoxically,
H 'achieves the finest articulation of his existential statement
within the content of the Romantic tradition'. Such visionary
poems offer a positive response to the modern experience.
Discusses principally 'The Darkling Thrush', 'At the Railway
Station, Upway', 'Old Furniture', 'At Castle Boterel', 'After
a Journey', 'The Phantom Horsewoman' and 'During Wind
and Rain'.

489 Hazen, James
'Hardy's War Poetry', *Four Decades of Poetry, 1890–1930*
2:2 (1978) 76–93

Thorough survey of H's war poems, noting their increasingly
critical and dark attitude and the deepening recognition of
war's importance in human history.

490 Holloway, John
' "No Answerer I" ', THE PROUD KNOWLEDGE:
POETRY, INSIGHT AND THE SELF, 1620–1920
(London: Routledge & Kegan Paul, 1977) 233–53

H was the first poet to be 'an almost encyclopaedic recorder
of everyday human life' and thus was the first 'genuinely
novelist-poet'. Holloway is mainly concerned here with
demonstrating how the poet or 'I' in the lyrics is, by the usual
standard of poetic character, 'a person of no account':
Hardy's role, one might say, is to be *'the poet as nobody'*. H's
finest lyrics are 'the heroic achievements of a poet whose role
was that of anti-hero'.

491 Howe, Irving
'The Short Poems of Thomas Hardy', *Southern Review* ns. 2
(October 1966) 878–905

Rather patronising view of the verse. Only a small portion of the poetry is distinguished, and H's origins and values are 'plebeian'. The 'Poems of 1912–13' succeed because H is 'supremely honest'.

492   Hynes, Samuel
'The Hardy Tradition in Modern English Poetry', THOMAS HARDY: THE WRITER AND HIS BACKGROUND, ed. Norman Page (London: Bell & Hyman, 1980) 173–91; reprinted in *Thomas Hardy Journal* 2:3 (October 1986) 32–49

Very rewarding, and often brilliant, definition of 'the Hardy tradition', with some brief remarks on his influence on later poets. The 'traditional' nature of H's verse is said to be thus: 'it is English and primarily concerned with actual nature and with man's relation to it; it is physical, not transcendental, but it is nevertheless religious in the sense that its nature is not "neutralized"; it is descriptive rather than metaphorical or symbolic; it is rooted in time, but not in history; it is often concerned with the reality of memory, and so is retrospective, sometimes regretful and melancholy, but also ironic and stoic; it observes the world, not the self. Formally, the tradition is conservative, but inventive.'

493   Hynes, Samuel
'On Hardy's Badnesses', ESSAYS ON AESTHETICS: PERSPECTIVES ON THE WORK OF MONROE C. BEARDSLEY, ed. John Fisher (Philadelphia: Temple University Press, 1983) 247–57

Absorbing thesis that H was two poets: 'one believed that poetry is an imitation of poetry, that it takes public and conventional forms', and when H thus attaches himself to the 'literary high culture' of his day, he is 'awful'. H's narrative, war, occasional and 'poetic' poems are the product of this poet. The other H regards poetry as 'an ordinary but private activity' with no audience or immediate precursors except 'anon., Hodge, and God'. It is this poet who writes the good H poems.

494   Ingham, Patricia
'Hardy and "The Cell of Time"', THE POETRY OF

THOMAS HARDY, ed. Patricia Clements and Juliet
Grindle (London: Vision Press, 1980) 119–36

Thematic survey of H's presentation of time which he shows
to be 'retrospective, denaturing, static, claustrophobic and
largely inescapable'. The poems of 1912–13, however, 'seem
to constitute stepping out of the cell'.

495   Johnson, Trevor
' "Pre-Critical Innocence" and the Anthologist's Hardy',
Victorian Poetry 17:1–2 (Spring–Summer 1979) 9–29

Challenges Leavis's view that H is a naïve, uncritical writer
by showing H's careful and continuing revision of 'During
Wind and Rain'. Leavis's belief that H wrote only a dozen or
so great poems is not borne out by a study of ten anthologies
of H's poetry; if Leavis were correct, surely all the great
poems would be in all the anthologies, but only two poems
achieve such status. (Appendix gives statistical analysis of
most anthologised poems.)

496   Johnson, H. A. Trevor
'Thomas Hardy and the Respectable Muse', THOMAS
HARDY YEAR BOOK No. 1 (1970) 27–42

Entertaining and shrewd lecture on H's reaction in his poetry
against Victorian taste and its fondness for escapist, moralising verse, as exemplified in apt quotations from Palgrave's
Golden Treasury. Nothing could be further from such homely
platitudes and coy evasions than H's 'full look at the Worst'.

497   Keith, W. J.
THE POETRY OF NATURE: RURAL PERSPECTIVES
IN POETRY FROM WORDSWORTH TO THE
PRESENT (Toronto, Buffalo, London: University of
Toronto Press, 1980)

Compelling attempt to place H in the tradition of 'nature'
poetry, stressing that in such poetry 'the subject seeing
proves at least as significant as the object seen'. Keith
demonstrates his view of poetic perspective in an analysis of
H's 'At Middle-Field Gate in February', which both records a
unique 'spot of time' and evokes a specific *genius loci*.

Excellent assessment of relationship with William Barnes, and detailed analysis of Wordsworthian features in H's poetic temperament. Acute close readings of a number of poems ('At Castle Boterel', 'The Fallow Deer at the Lonely House', 'The Sheep-Boy'). H is clearly a central figure in the kind of poetry which Keith discusses.

498   King, Kathryn R., and Morgan, William W.
'Hardy and the Boer War: The Public Poet in Spite of Himself', *Victorian Poetry* 17:1–2 (Spring–Summer 1979) 66–83

H 'regularly turned out poems concerned with issues of national moment', beginning with his eleven poems on the Boer War, which are 'surprisingly subversive of the war effort'. H is here 'a public poet skeptical of the power of public utterance to bring about any real change'. H speaks as an unhappy member of a culture, refusing either to endorse its values or 'self-righteously declare his superiority to them'. His public voice thus shares 'the strange loneliness, tentativeness, and staunchness' of all his best poems.

499   Leavis, F. R.
'Hardy the Poet', *Southern Review,* Thomas Hardy Centennial Edition 6 (Summer 1940) 87–98

Reiterates and supplements his earlier contentions and reservations about H's poetry. 'Lack of distinction in Hardy becomes a positive quality.'

500   Leavis, F. R.
NEW BEARINGS IN ENGLISH POETRY: A STUDY OF THE CONTEMPORARY SITUATION (London: Chatto & Windus, 1932) 52–62

Oracular dismissal of H the poet as an outdated Victorian whose 'solidity appears archaic'. H is 'a naïve poet of simple attitudes and outlook' and, though he felt deeply and communicated it perfectly in his best poems, 'his originality was not of the kind that goes with a high degree of critical awareness'. His rank as a major poet rests on a dozen poems. 'Hardy's great poetry is a triumph of character. Now and then, when he is deeply moved (the impulse is usually a poignant memory), . . . the oddity becomes an intensely personal virtue.' (There follows praise of 'The Voice'.) Usually, though, the main impulse behind his verse is 'the mere impulse to write verse'.

501   Lewis, Cecil Day
'The Lyrical Poetry of Thomas Hardy', *Proceedings of the British Academy* 37 (1951) 155–74: The Warton Lecture on English Poetry, delivered 6 June 1951; reprinted as book with same title (London: Cumberledge, 1957). Substantial extracts in Gibson and Johnson (eds.), A CASEBOOK (429) 147–60

Excellent defence of H's poetry, insisting that 'personality must enter any discussion of Hardy's verse', for his technique becomes masterly only when he writes of personal experience. The best of his verse, because the most personal, are the 'Poems of 1912–13', with their underlying 'good bone, formed by the sincerity, the refusal to overstate an emotion or falsify a situation'. This is a poet's appreciation of H, sharp, moving and very readable.

502   Lewis, Cecil Day
'The Shorter Poems of Thomas Hardy', *Bell,* Dublin 8 (September 1944) 513–25

An astute appraisal of H's 'deliberate roughness' and his technical skill. There are many dull poems but the best testify to the struggle between conformity and the unorthodox imagination.

503   Lucas, John
'Thomas Hardy, Donald Davie, England and the English', THOMAS HARDY ANNUAL No. 1, ed. Norman Page (London: Macmillan, 1982) 134–51

A combative and aggressive account of Donald Davie's *Thomas Hardy and British Poetry* (427) which Lucas regards as tendentious and procrustean in its depiction of H as the modest liberal whose 'acceptance of the second-best' has diverted modern poetry away from radical confrontation with major issues. To Lucas, however, H's 'modes of acceptance amount to a comprehending generosity of vision that seems to me far more valuable for English poetry than the alternatives that Davie prescribes'.

504   McCarthy, Robert
'Hardy and "The Lonely Burden of Consciousness": The Poet's Flirtation with the Void', *English Literature in Transition* 23:2 (1980) 89–98

H's poetry may be superficially Victorian, but it has also an 'undeniable modernity' in its conflict between conscious and unconscious forces. H shows that to withdraw from a world of tragic sensitivity into one of the unsophisticated and unconscious may be a nostalgic retreat, but it is in reality a kind of self-entombment.

505   Mahar, Margaret
'Hardy's Poetry of Renunciation', *Journal of English Literary History* 45 (1978) 303–24

In the lyric poem, H found his freedom from the burden of the novel's Aristotelian plot and the temporal sequence of narrative. 'The poems are quite self-consciously not monuments which by representing a life or an epoch stand as bulwarks against the ongoingness of time; the lyrics do not aspire to the novel's bulk. Their strength lies elsewhere, in their renunciation, a refusal of realism, which is for Hardy a refusal of both illusion and disillusion.' His one true belief is a belief in dualism, the 'doubling of perspective, rhyme, and metaphor, an irreconcilable doubling in time which his poetry does not wish to overcome'. [Especially good on 'During Wind and Rain' and 'Under the Waterfall'.]

506   Marken, Ronald
'"As Rhyme Meets Rhyme" in the Poetry of Thomas Hardy', THE POETRY OF THOMAS HARDY, ed. Patricia Clements and Juliet Grindle (London: Vision Press, 1980) 18–32

Fascinating prosodic analyses and close readings of a number of poems which define H's 'accents of remorse'. The effects of H's use of rhyme range through 'the bizarre, brash, humorous, plain, and predictable to the deft and exquisitely subtle'.

507   Martin, Graham and Furbank, P. N. (eds)
TWENTIETH CENTURY POETRY: CRITICAL ESSAYS
AND DOCUMENTS (Milton Keynes: Open University
Press, 1975) 257–69, 269–80

Reprints excerpts from William H. Pritchard (523) and
Douglas Brown (117).

508   Morgan, William W.
'The Partial Vision: Hardy's Idea of Dramatic Poetry',
Tennessee Studies in Literature 20 (1975) 100–8; reprinted in
Gibson and Johnson (eds), A CASEBOOK (429) 244–52

In his impersonal poems, H often effaces his narrator and in
his personal poems he 'binds his narrator's vision to the
moment so as to restrict its relevance to the particulars in the
poem'. Both have a kind of incompleteness of vision which
seeks to prevent direct self-revelation.

509   Neuman, S. C.
' "Emotion Put into Measure": Meaning in Hardy's Poetry',
THE POETRY OF THOMAS HARDY, ed. Patricia
Clements and Juliet Grindle (London: Vision Press, 1980)
33–51

Excellent prosodic analyses of selected poems (especially
'The Master and the Leaves'), showing how prosody can
convey, in its own right, a 'rational content', which can reveal
what the lexis leaves unsaid or can contradict it.

510   Orel, Harold
'After *The Dynasts:* Hardy's Relationship to Christianity',
BUDMOUTH ESSAYS ON THOMAS HARDY [etc. – see
103] 180–91

In the verse of his final years which deals with Christianity, H
appears 'self-convinced, humanely sceptical' and occasionally
regretful.

511   Orel, Harold
'Hardy, War, and the Years of *Pax Britannica*', THOMAS
HARDY AND THE MODERN WORLD (104) 90–105

Provocative study of H's war poetry, arguing that, in the last decade of his life, H renounced his faith in 'the powers of reason, science, and the evolving consciousness of the Immanent Will to create a better world'.

512   Ousby, Ian
'Past and Present in Hardy's "Poems of Pilgrimage" ',
Victorian Poetry 17:1–2 (Spring–Summer 1979) 51–64

These poems present an 'extended meditation on the European past', the contemplation of history reminding him of 'the long record of human suffering' and the hopelessly tragic nature of the human condition. For the artist, however, contemplation of the past is essential in that it leads to moments of vision which are 'the very core of poetic creativity'.

513   Partridge, A. C.
THE LANGUAGE OF MODERN POETRY: YEATS,
ELIOT, AUDEN (London: André Deutsch, 1976) 12, 33,
35–9, 53, 260, 327

Sensitive defence of H's poetic language, stressing that his rhythms are natural and that his monologues have fewer sudden transitions than those of Robert Browning.

514   Paulin, Tom
'Time and Sense Experience: Hardy and T. S. Eliot',
BUDMOUTH ESSAYS ON THOMAS HARDY [etc. – see
103] 192–204

On the cruelties and tyrannies of time in H's verse. Memory was the way open to H of preserving existence but is itself subject to time. Eliot seeks beyond time for some transcendental substitute, but his rejection, even detestation, of sense experience makes him a much more negative poet than H, for whom 'the knowledge derived from experience – empirical knowledge – is all there is'.

515   Paulin, Tom
' "Words, in all their intimate accents" ', THOMAS
HARDY ANNUAL No. 1, ed. Norman Page (London:
Macmillan, 1982) 84–94

A combative plea to consider the voice, or voices, of H's poetry, rather than the patterns of visual images. H is said to write in the Gothic tradition, which has 'a thorny fricative texture, lacks sonority, smoothness, and obviously regular metre, and is intimately keyed to all the shifts and changes in the speaking voice'. H possesses an 'intimately vocal aesthetic', and his conception of poetic accent incorporates not just stress and emphasis, but also a spoken provincial accent 'nurtured in the depths of a rural folk culture'. Paulin gives many brief, conclusive examples, and his engaged, contentious tone makes this a thoroughly readable article.

516 Peck, John
'Hardy and the Figure in the Scene', *Agenda* 10:2–3
(Spring–Summer 1972) 117–25

H 'stage-manages many of his landscape moments' in his poetry with a cinematic care as a way of 'composing the ironies of obsessive memory'. The compulsive subject is thus viewed with careful control, permitting the conversion of sadness into wisdom. Close readings of half a dozen poems.

517 Peck, John
'Pound and Hardy', *Agenda* 10:2–3 (Spring–Summer 1972)
3–10

On Pound's admiration for H's poetry.

518 Perkins, David
'Hardy and the Poetry of Isolation', *Journal of English
Literary History* 26 (June 1959) 253–70; partly reprinted in
Albert J. Guerard (ed.) (93) 143–59

In H's poems, mind or awareness is a uniquely human possession, and 'the fact of consciousness itself is the ground of human isolation in the cosmos'. The protagonists in the lyrics are often old men alone in their memories or lovers acutely ignorant of the heart of their partners. In his obsessive attention to the processes of memory, H dramatised 'the subjective isolation of the individual', for the content of memory is inevitably personal.

H recognizes two ways of escaping such isolation: resigned unawareness and the visionary imagination. 'Both of these roads are blocked for Hardy by his helpless honesty to his own experience, which he can neither elude nor transform.'

[Detailed discussion of 'The Man He Killed', 'The Darkling Thrush', 'The Impercipient' and 'In a Whispering Gallery'.]

519   Pinsky, Robert
'Hardy, Ransom, Berryman: A "Curious Air"'', *Agenda* 10:2–3 (Spring–Summer 1972) 89–99

On H's poetic 'oddities' of style and his 'self-deflation, an impatience with certain elegant and traditional ways of writing which the poet has mastered but mistrusts'.

520   Pinto, Vivian de Sola
'Hardy and Housman', CRISIS IN ENGLISH POETRY, 1880–1940 (London: Hutchinson, 1951) 36–58

An enthusiastic general introduction to the poetry, in which H overcomes the modern crisis by making it explicit and giving 'poetic form to a tragic vision of life reflected in the modern consciousness'.

521   Porter, Katherine Anne
'Notes on a Criticism of Thomas Hardy', *Southern Review,* Thomas Hardy Centennial Edition 6 (Summer 1940) 150–61; reprinted in Ian Watt (ed.) (108) 390–400

Challenges T. S. Eliot's dismissal of H in *After Strange Gods* (693), and places his unorthodoxies in a tradition of plain-styled dissent. H's characters 'suffer the tragedy of being, Eliot's by not being'.

522   Pound, Ezra
ABC OF READING (London: Faber & Faber, 1951) 193

Many clever people have wrongly ignored H's poetry: 'it is only maturer patience that can sweep aside a writer's honest error, and overlook unaccomplished clumsiness or outlandishness or old-fashionedness, for the sake of the solid centre'.

523   Pritchard, William H.
'Hardy's Anonymous Sincerity', *Agenda* 10:2–3
(Spring–Summer 1972) 100–16

The anonymous and un-personal voice in many of H's poems
explains why a reader 'often feels excitingly free in the
voice's presence, yet knows not where to turn for the final
guidance that voice refuses to give him'. Truth, honesty and
sincerity are not adequate descriptions of poems which make
no concessions to the reader and provide no cues for
responding to their 'odd kind of directness'.
    Pages 100–12 are reprinted in TWENTIETH CENTURY
POETRY: CRITICAL ESSAYS AND DOCUMENTS, ed.
Graham Martin and P. N. Furbank (507) 257–69.

524   Pritchard, William H.
'Hardy's Winter Words', *Hudson Review* 32:3 (Autumn
1979) 369–97

Urbane, readable and wide-ranging introduction to H's
poetry, surveying the whole of his career and not pursuing
any particular thesis. Some excellent analyses of individual
poems.

525   Quinn, Maire A.
'The Personal Past in the Poetry of Thomas Hardy and
Edward Thomas', *Critical Quarterly* 16:1 (Spring 1974) 7–28

Sees H as a Victorian poet. Focuses on H's 'poetry of
haunting' which is 'constructed around the possibility of a
transitory, brief and uncertain recovery of the personal past',
a recovery denied entirely to the modern Thomas. Good
analyses of 'Poems of 1912–13'. Devotes more individual
attention to H than Dollimore (475), but pursues a simpler
thesis.

526   Ransom, John Crowe
'Honey and Gall', *Southern Review,* Thomas Hardy
Centennial Edition 6 (Summer 1940) 1–19

Rather diffuse and depreciating. H's ironic poems are
praised, but generally he is seen here as a 'great minor poet'.

527   Richards, I. A.
'Some Notes on Hardy's Verse Forms', *Victorian Poetry*
17:1–2 (Spring–Summer 1979) 1–8

Acute comments on the variety of themes and treatment.
Especially interesting on how 'one or more phrases will
suddenly release a flood of hitherto unsuspected meaning'
(examples given from 'The Voice').

528   Robinson, Peter
'In Another's Words: Thomas Hardy's Poetry', *English* 31
(1982) 221–46

Examines some related qualities in H's verse: 'regular and
irregular rhythms and stanza forms; the unforeseen in human
experience, and the predestined or fated; and then, quoted
or spoken words within inverted commas and the stanza form
they fit'. Illuminating comments on 'Poems of 1912–13'.

529   Schwartz, Delmore
'Poetry and Belief in Thomas Hardy', *Southern Review,*
Thomas Hardy Centennial Edition 6 (Summer 1940) 64–77;
reprinted in Albert J. Guerard (ed.) (93) 123–34

H's 'state of mind is one example of the conflict between the
new scientific view of Life which the nineteenth century
produced and the whole attitude toward Life which had been
traditional to Western culture. Hardy is a partisan of the new
view, but acutely conscious always of the old view. He holds
the two in a dialectical tension.' H failed when he tried to
state his beliefs directly, but 'he succeeded when he used his
beliefs to make significant the observations which concerned
him'.

530   Shilstone, Frederick W.
'Conversing Stances in Hardy's Shorter Poems', *Colby
Library Quarterly* 12:3 (September 1976) 139–48

The various 'voices' which are heard in H's shorter lyrics
allow H to express a contradictory and unresolved response
to the world. The three main voices in H's 'aesthetic
dialogue' are those of the ironist, the myth-making observer
of a personal past and the ageing realist.

531   Siemens, Lloyd G.
        'Hardy's Poetry and the Rhetoric of Negation', *Dalhousie Review* 58:1 (Spring 1978), 69–78

        Seeks to qualify the view that the antinomial pattern (thesis set against antithesis to produce an unresolved ironic complex) is the only or most characteristic pattern in H's poetry. (See Hynes, 430.) Indeed, many of the apparently antinomial poems lack ironic tension, for the thesis is negated and undercut, expectation being abruptly followed by unfulfilment or reality. Siemens proceeds to illustrate this 'consistent pattern and tone of negation' in a number of poems.

532   Sisson, C. H.
        'Hardy and Barnes', *Agenda* 10:2–3 (Spring–Summer 1972) 47–9

        H used the Dorset poet, Wiliam Barnes, as a touchstone for his own poetry, especially the latter's ' "closeness of phrase to his vision" '. Interesting reflections on the use of dialect in poetry.

533   Stallworthy, Jon
        'Read by Moonlight', THE POETRY OF THOMAS HARDY, ed. Patricia Clements and Juliet Grindle (London: Vision Press, 1980) 172–87

        Traces H's use of moon imagery to express 'love betrayed, eclipsed, or suffering'.

534   Steele, Jeremy V.
        'Thoughts from Sophocles: Hardy in the '90s', THE POETRY OF THOMAS HARDY, ed. Patricia Clements and Juliet Grindle (London: Vision Press, 1980) 69–82

        Chiefly explains the influence of Sophocles' *Oedipus Rex* on H's poetry. The Oedipus plays provided H with 'images of his own distress'.

535   Swigg, Richard
        'Hardy's "Even Monochrome and Curving Line" ', *Agenda* 10:2–3 (Spring–Summer 1972) 81–8

Close readings of eight poems, showing how H achieves a precise focus on suffering by refusing to 'transgress the limits of his consciousness' and by willing 'a sensibility where several responses have been numbed, blanked out'.

536   Symons, Arthur
'Thomas Hardy', *Dial* 68 (January 1920) 66–70

Acute praise of H's poetry, which speaks 'in a slow, twisted, and sometimes enigmatic manner, without obvious charm, but with some arresting quality'. H is a profoundly interesting poet with sap in his veins, rather than blood.

537   Tate, Allen
'Hardy's Philosophic Metaphors', *Southern Review,* Thomas Hardy Centennial Edition 6 (Summer 1940) 99–108

Clearly prefers the less philosophical verse where there is none of that 'ill-digested' blend of naturalism, deism and theism. H's intellectual position often contradicts his poetic feeling.

538   Taylor, Dennis
'The Patterns in Hardy's Poetry', *Journal of English Literary History* 42 (1975) 258–75

Suggestive essay, copiously illustrated, shows that H deliberately dramatises 'how patterns of experience develop' and grow rigid, becoming vulnerable to 'the jar of new and unseen life'. H is very far from merely imposing rigid frames upon experience.

539   Taylor, Dennis
'The Riddle of Hardy's Poetry', *Victorian Poetry* 11 (1973) 262–76

Important attempt to explain why H's poems, for all their defects, can have such emotional impact. The defects are transmuted by a 'meditative reverie' and H 'dramatizes how fresh expressions grow archaic in time and how imaginative insights grow abstract and doctrinaire'. It is thus the oddity of the verse that 'when Hardy's poetry is "transmuted" and becomes "sincere", his *idées fixes,* his obsolete words – in sum, the rigid architecture of his verse – become somehow consistent with a world in process'. [Extended analysis of 'Copying Architecture in an Old Minster', 'The Phantom Horsewoman', 'During Wind and Rain' and 'A Light Snow-Fall After Frost'.]

540 Taylor, Dennis
'Victorian Philology and Victorian Poetry', *Victorian Newsletter* 53 (Spring 1978) 13–16

Both H and Hopkins were influenced by Victorian philology in their use of experimental language and archaisms. H is aware of the 'gloomy paradox' that such language contradicts his preference for the ' "real language of men" '.

541 Wain, John
'The Poetry of Thomas Hardy', *Critical Quarterly* 8 (1966) 166–73; reprinted as Introduction to SELECTED SHORTER POEMS OF THOMAS HARDY (London: Macmillan; New York: St Martin's Press, 1966) ix–xix

An enthusiastic but patronising introduction. 'We are in the presence of what can only be called a peasant view of life', and 'when Hardy lashes out in sudden anger, it is like a blow from a navvy's fist'. None of the poems, though, is 'quite without interest'. Compare Raymond Williams' denial that H is a peasant (675).

542 Wilson, Keith
'The Personal Voice in the Poetry of Thomas Hardy', BUDMOUTH ESSAYS ON THOMAS HARDY [etc. – see 103] 205–17

On the theoretical assumptions which underlie H's role as a spokesman for the personal voice in poetry. Many quotations from his second *Literary Notebook.*

543 Wright, David
'Notes on Hardy', *Agenda* 10:2–3 (Spring–Summer 1972) 66–73

A series of brief, aphoristic observations on H and his poetry. Often acute or contentious; useful essay titles here.

544   Zietlow, Paul
'Thomas Hardy – Poet', THE VICTORIAN
EXPERIENCE: THE POETS, ed. Richard A. Levine
(Ohio: Ohio University Press, 1982) 178–202

Introductory survey of the poetry, stressing H's stance as a 'chronicler of the world' rather than an 'imaginative singer'.

The Dynasts

545   Abercrombie, Lascelles
'Thomas Hardy's *The Dynasts*', *Proceedings of the Royal Institution of Great Britain* 29, Part 3 (1936) 444–62

Regards the poem as H's greatest single achievement. Abercrombie's infectious enthusiasm does not blind him to the work's defects, however: the poem's greatness lies 'in its imagination; not in the craftsmanship by which his imagination is wrought into language'.

546   Bailey, J. O.
THOMAS HARDY AND THE COSMIC MIND (Chapel Hill, N.C.: University of North Carolina Press; London: Oxford University Press, 1956)

Principally concerned to examine the Spirits in the context of Eduard Von Hartmann's theory of the Unconscious. The conclusion endorses the poem's view that 'evolutionary meliorism is possible, that the consciousness may be striving to express itself'. Includes a scholarly reappraisal of the Immanent Will.

547   Dean, Susan
HARDY'S POETIC VISION IN *THE DYNASTS:* THE DIORAMA OF A DREAM (Princeton, N.J., and Guildford: Princeton University Press, 1977)

Probably the best book-length study of *D* and offers a strong defence of the poem. Dean draws an analogy with the diorama (a Victorian optical exhibit which gave illusions of perspective and depth) to illustrate *D*'s fascination with receding planes of reality and different modes of vision. In *D,* she believes, H 'not only presents an action, the war with Napoleon, but in addition represents the watching of that action: a double show'. Many of the problems which *D* poses for the reader (lack of immediacy, flat characters, convoluted style) do not stem from H's ineptitude but from his deliberate aesthetic and his desire to show 'vision in action', a vision which refuses to ignore the peripheral or the deflating.

548   Dobrée, Bonamy
'The Dynasts', Southern Review, Thomas Hardy Centennial Edition 6 (Summer 1940) 109–24

While not blind to the poem's weaknesses, Dobrée gives a sympathetic analysis, stressing the use of microscopic close-ups and panoramic surveys.

549   Friedman, Barton R.
'Proving Nothing: History and Dramatic Strategy in *The Dynasts', CLIO: A Journal of Literary History and the Philosophy of History* 13 (1984) 101–22

Discusses how H transforms the chaotic facts of history into an heroic myth of Albion. The spirits have many diverse responses to the Napoleonic drama, stressing H's view of the Immanent Will as impenetrable mystery, lacking humanly rational motives. The Spirits are only explorations of the possibilities for making sense and order out of the seemingly chaotic nature of history, and to that extent they 'prove nothing'.

550   Garrison, Chester A.
THE VAST VENTURE: HARDY'S EPIC-DRAMA 'THE DYNASTS', Salzburg Studies in English Literature 18 (Salzburg: Institut für Englische Sprache und Literatur, 1973)

Discusses the poem's reception, sources, analogues, historical contents, style and relation to the novels.

551   Horsman, E. A.
'The Language of *The Dynasts', Durham University Journal* ns. 10 (December 1948), 11–16

A detailed analysis of H's archaisms, dialects, colloquial and scientific words. Concludes that the poem succeeds in spite of its language.

552 Jones, Lawrence
'Thomas Hardy's "Idiosyncratic Mode of Regard"', *Journal of English Literary History* 42 (1975) 433–59

Principally on H's personal vision in the seemingly 'impersonal' *D*. H's unique mode of seeing is detached and spectatorial, with shifting perspectives. Detailed analysis of H's omniscient narration.

553 Morcos, Louis
'*The Dynasts* and the Bible', *Bulletin of English Studies,* Cairo, Egypt (1950) 29–65

While *D* is obviously not a Christian epic, H nevertheless employs many Biblical allusions, especially from the Old Testament. The Book of Job, for instance, makes an ironic analogue to the action of *D*, which lacks any 'direct mutual relationships between man and the universe'.

554 Morcos, Louis
'The Manuscript of Thomas Hardy's *The Dynasts*', *Annals of the Faculty of Arts,* Ain Shams University, Cairo, Egypt 3 (January 1955) 1–39

On H's revisions, showing his increasingly clear and optimistic perception of the poem's philosophy.

555 Orel, Harold
THOMAS HARDY'S EPIC DRAMA: A STUDY OF *THE DYNASTS* (Lawrence, Kansas: University of Kansas Press, 1963)

Most interesting in its comparison of *D* with other epics, showing its deviation from Homer and Milton in its invention of celestial machinery, the 'pitiful stature' of its central character, its inability to give a happy ending, and its abhorrence of war. In such ways, *D* is a 'frank divergence from classical and other dramatic precedent'.

556 Orel, Harold
'What *The Dynasts* Meant to Hardy', *Victorian Poetry* 17:1–2 (Spring–Summer 1979) 109–23

Enthusiastic and animated account of H's aims in writing *D* which 'triumphs over its faults' in its 'splendor of vision unique to Hardy'. [Originally published as introduction to the New Wessex edition of *The Dynasts,* ed. Harold Orel (London: Macmillan, 1978).]

557   Stedmond, J. M.
'Hardy's *Dynasts* and Mythical Method', *English* 12 (Spring 1958) 1–4

H may have employed an Aeschylean structure in *D*, but it is used *ironically,* since Aeschylus's moral order is the product of a just deity, while H's order derives from an apparently purposeless Will. Stedmond makes H sound quite Joycean at times.

558   Wain, John
'Introduction', *The Dynasts,* ed. John Wain (New York: St Martin's Press, 1965) v–xix

Regards *D* in cinematic terms as a shooting-script. The poem has serious faults, not least the sheer variety of verse forms which makes it appear that H is regarding the writing as a hobby, rather like 'collecting sea-shells'.

559   Wickens, G. Glen
'Hardy's Inconsistent Spirits and the Philosophic Form of *The Dynasts*', THE POETRY OF THOMAS HARDY, ed. Patricia Clements and Juliet Grindle (London: Vision Press, 1980) 101–18

In his epic poem, H attempted to 'open up reality outside the prison of mechanistic determinism' by emphasising the need for a philosophy of perspectives that can render the many, not yet fully understood, aspects of nature. *D*'s greatness is that it 'unquestionably asserts the belief that if evolution is to have any meaning and goal, modern man must ultimately be beyond irony and a paralysis of the will'.

560   Wilson, Keith
' "Flower of Man's Intelligence": World and Overworld in

The Dynasts', Victorian Poetry 17:1–2 (Spring–Summer
1979) 124–33

Wilson opposes 'horizontal' readings of *D*, which place the
spirits 'up there' and the humans below, preferring a
'vertical' reading which 'connects particular Spirits with their
obvious human counterparts'. These connecting strands make
D a tightly structured work, a 'secular epic' in which 'human
nature, abstracted into a number of simplified essences,
occupies the place traditionally taken by a divine pantheon'.
Man is both world and overworld in *D*.

561 Wilson, K. G.
'Hardy's *The Dynasts*: Some Problems of Interpretation',
Colby Library Quarterly, 12:4 (December 1976) 181–90

The 'philosophy' of *D* may be optimistic, but, as a work of
literature, it 'remains pervaded by despair'. This distinction
explains the divided critical reaction to *D*.

562 Wright, Walter F.
THE SHAPING OF *THE DYNASTS:* A STUDY IN
THOMAS HARDY (Lincoln: University of Nebraska Press,
1967)

A scrupulous and thoroughly researched account of the
origins, evolution and composition of *D*; a valuable source of
H's previously unpublished notes, etc. Displays the breadth
and eclectic nature of H's reading while stressing his imaginative synthesis of such material.

General Hardy Themes and Areas of Criticism

Darwin and science

563 Asker, D. B. D.
' "The Birds *Shall* Have Some Dinner": Animals in Hardy's
Fiction', *Dutch Quarterly Review of Anglo-American Letters*
10:3 (1980) 215–19

Suggests Darwinian influence on H's hatred of animal
suffering. Chiefly on *T* and *JO*, where the pain of the animals
parallels that of the protagonists.

564 Bailey, J. O.
'Hardy's "Imbedded Fossil" ', *Studies in Philology* 42 (July
1945) 663–74

On H's many allusions to science.

565 Bailey, J. O.
'Heredity as Villain in the Poetry and Fiction of Thomas
Hardy', THOMAS HARDY YEAR BOOK No. 1 (1970)
9–19

Discusses H's interest in heredity as demonstrated in *T, JO*
and four poems ('Heredity', 'The Pedigree', 'Sine Prole' and
'Family Portraits'). Makes the rather exaggerated claim that,
in *T* and *JO*, the 'basic forces explaining character and
governing the action are genetic'.

566 Beer, Gillian
'Finding a Scale for the Human: Plot and Writing in Hardy's
Novels', DARWIN'S PLOTS: EVOLUTIONARY
NARRATIVE IN DARWIN, GEORGE ELIOT AND
NINETEENTH-CENTURY FICTION (London: Routledge
& Kegan Paul, 1983) 236–58

Likens H's tragic or malign plots to the determinism of
Darwin's natural selection, paining the reader by 'the sense

of multiple possibilities, only one of which can occur'. Also gives a more general discussion of H's response to Darwinism, especially the problems of finding 'a scale for the human, and a place for the human within the natural order'.

567 Brogan, Howard O.
'Science and Narrative Structure in Austen, Hardy, and Woolf', *Nineteenth-Century Fiction* 11:4 (March 1957) 276–87

H's philosophy derives in part from mechanistic science, and he manipulates the plot of *MC* to demonstrate his theory of deterministic tragedy, refusing to offer any healing catharsis.

568 Cosslett, Tess
THE 'SCIENTIFIC MOVEMENT' AND VICTORIAN LITERATURE (Brighton, Sussex: Harvester Press; New York: St Martin's Press, 1982) 132–68

Rewarding survey of H's attitude to science. Long analysis of the cliff-hanging scene in *PBE*, and useful comments on Fitzpiers in *W*. H remains largely reductive and pessimistic: 'for Hardy, the scientific fact of our physical bond to Nature does not expand into an overall coherent scientific vision of relationship and oneness.' Earlier chapters discuss Tennyson, George Eliot and Meredith.

569 Ebbatson, Roger
THE EVOLUTIONARY SELF: HARDY, FORSTER, LAWRENCE (Brighton, Sussex: Harvester Press, 1982)

Ebbatson comments on H and Darwinism. In *FMC* social forces of change which are inconvenient to H's middle-class readers are edited out, but in *W* and the later novels these are presented more honestly.

570 Orel, Harold
'Hardy and the Developing Science of Archaeology', THOMAS HARDY ANNUAL No. 4, ed. Norman Page (London: Macmillan, 1986) 19–44

Demonstrates that H 'would not have shaped the specific philosophy that he did, if the intellectual excitement created by increasingly serious investigators in several hard sciences – geology, biology, and archaeology, among others' had not influenced him. Discusses especially *PBE, T, MC, RN* and *A Group of Noble Dames*.

571   Robinson, Roger
'Hardy and Darwin', THOMAS HARDY: THE WRITER AND HIS BACKGROUND, ed. Norman Page (London: Bell & Hyman, 1980) 128–50

Beginning from the thesis that H never lost 'his deep initial belief in the absolute truthfulness and the fundamental hopelessness of Darwin's ideas', Robinson shows how H responds to Darwin's 'depressive revelations' about loss, instability, incoherence and the reduction of human significance. Extensive discussion of *T*, regarded here as the greatest work of the Darwinian crisis.

Narrative technique

572   Andersen, Carol Reed
'Time, Space, and Perspective in Thomas Hardy', *Nineteenth-Century Fiction* 9:3 (December 1954) 192–208

Important defence of H's metaphorical form, which embodies his central perspective of the concurrence of past and present. H's unique achievement lies in his manner of interweaving metaphorical equivalents of a dominating theme. Disusses *FMC, RN* and *T*.

573   Anderson, Wayne C.
'The Rhetoric of Silence in Hardy's Fiction', *Studies in the Novel* 17 (1985) 53–68

Early chapters of *RN* are analysed to show how H uses silence and withholding of information as 'a strategy for eliciting our own acts of interpretation as readers'. The minor characters are noisy, but H himself is silent and detached, forcing us to interpret more actively. Though H eventually breaks his silences, the delay obliges us to 'cunningly enlarge the particulars of Hardy's silences to create satisfactory readings of our own'. Innovative reader-response approach.

574   Buckler, William E.
THE VICTORIAN IMAGINATION: ESSAYS IN
AESTHETIC EXPLORATION (Brighton, Sussex:
Harvester Press, 1980) 297–376

Four chapters reprint previously published articles on 'Poems of 1912–13' (440) (mythical subtexts permit H to gain distance from complex emotions), *D* (two chapters on the extraordinary aesthetic adventure of reading this epic poem) and on 'Thomas Hardy's Illusion of Letters'. (H 'created the illusion of total availability to anyone who could read'. Chiefly on *D*, *T* and *JO*.)

575   Carpenter, Richard C.
'Hardy's "Gurgoyles" ', *Modern Fiction Studies* 6 (Autumn 1960) 223–32

H's use of the grotesque (e.g. the gargoyle in *FMC*) contributes to his 'anti-realism' by enriching and thickening the 'aesthetic texture'. Such dissonance serves a thematic purpose in revealing 'the morass beneath'.

576   Davidson, Donald
'The Traditional Basis of Thomas Hardy's Fiction', *Southern Review*, Thomas Hardy Centennial Edition 6 (Summer 1940) 162–78; reprinted in Albert J. Guerard (ed.) (93) 10–23

H wrote 'as a ballad-maker would write if a ballad-maker were to have to write novels'. He works in a folk tradition, not a literary one, with its emphasis on action, not psychology, and its use of character archetypes.

577   Fleishman, Avrom
THE ENGLISH HISTORICAL NOVEL: WALTER
SCOTT TO VIRGINIA WOOLF (Baltimore and London:
Johns Hopkins University Press, 1971) 179–207

Studies *TM*, *T* and *D* as examples of H's 'originality in historical fiction', especially his systematic rejection of both

Romanticism and Historicism. It is in *T* where H most nearly approaches the role of a historical novelist, creating a 'symbolic model of the pattern of British historical experience' and examining 'the sources of value buried in pre-history'.

578   Forster, E. M.
ASPECTS OF THE NOVEL (London: Edward Arnold; New York: Harcourt, Brace, 1927) 140–2, 198

H is essentially a poet who conceives of his novels 'from an enormous height'. Except with Tess, he expects his characters to acquiesce in the plot and its emphasis on causality. While 'the fate above us, not the fate working through us' is most memorable in the Wessex novels, the characters are enchained by cause and effect, and the plot consequently 'never catches humanity in its teeth'. In *D*, however, H's success is complete because he establishes complete contact between the plot and the actors.

579   Friedman, Alan
'Thomas Hardy: "Weddings Be Funerals"', THE TURN OF THE NOVEL (London: Oxford University Press, 1966) 38–74

Charts H's development from the traditional form of the closed ending to the open and expanding ending. The ending of *FMC* is closed, Bathsheba's desolation being contained and confined by her marriage to Oak. *T,* however, is written as a 'resistlessly expanding form of personal experience' (her movement towards disintegration), although the contrived tragic resolution of the final chapter may appear to compromise this. It is in *JO* that H completes his attack on the conventional ending, for Jude's 'formal remarriage and death provide no resolution but merely leave open his progress towards moral disintegration'. A fascinating and convincing study of the three novels.

580   Hardy, Barbara
TELLERS AND LISTENERS: THE NARRATIVE IMAGINATION (London: The Athlone Press, University of London, 1975) 175–205

Barbara Hardy focuses on the telling of tales within H's novels and what these reveal not only of the characters of the tellers, but also of the communal circumstances in which such story-telling takes place and of the charitable, though caustic, nature of H's own narrative attitude. Clearly written, sensitive and illuminated with well-chosen comparisons.

581 Hawkins, Desmond
     'The Strategy of the Novelist', BUDMOUTH ESSAYS ON
     THOMAS HARDY [etc. – see 103] 9–20

Concentrates on H's technique in the early novels, especially *FMC*. Notes H's unifying theme, detached panoramic vision, command of volcanic emotion, especially sexual passion, and the contrasting of rural scenes and voices with the violence of the drama.

582 Hynes, Samuel
     'Hardy's Historians', THOMAS HARDY ANNUAL No. 5,
     ed. Norman Page (London: Macmillan, 1987) 102–18

H's Prefaces to his novels urge us to read them *historically,* as novels about 'history-as-process – the nature of social change, the forces that generate change, and the effects of change on human lives. Historical change is the *reality* of the novels, the medium in which the action flows.' H's historians include the narrator, locating the tale in time and space, as well as characters who are parish historians, and personal historians, his central tragic characters whose tragedies *are* their histories.

583 Jacobus, Mary
     'Hardy's Magian Retrospect', *Essays in Criticism* 32 (1982)
     258–79

Encounters or dialogues between H and his ghostly other self show his concern with immortality and speaking from the grave. His characteristic mode of irony is therefore temporal, looking before and after at any given moment. When this irony slips and H is unable to see himself as anything but a ghost from the past, we have a sudden upsurge of imaginative energy in the form of the grotesque, the anarchic overwhelming of the perceiver. Such critical moments occur in *PBE*, *FMC* and *WB*.

584   Jones, Lawrence O.
'Imitation and Expression in Thomas Hardy's Theory of Fiction', *Studies in the Novel* 7:4 (Winter 1975) 507–25

H reconciles imitation and expression in his working aesthetic. He emphasises the expressive view of art as the projection of an individual temperament but stresses the need to transcend limitations of personal vision and gain access to the 'heart and inner meaning' of reality. Interesting on H's similarities with French Impressionists and J. M. W. Turner.

585   Kincaid, James R.
'Hardy's Absences', CRITICAL APPROACHES TO THE FICTION OF THOMAS HARDY, ed. Dale Kramer (London: Macmillan, 1979) 202–14

H's narratives are not indeterminate but rather formally incoherent; they present us with quite clear organising patterns, but these are multiple and contradictory so that the narratives create 'definite but incompatible expectations, not exactly frustrating any set of expectations but refusing to allow us to fulfil our rage for order and coherence by satisfying any one set of expectations exclusively'. Detailed study of the pig-killing scene in *JO* and the cliff-hanging episode in *PBE*.

586   King, Jeannette
TRAGEDY IN THE VICTORIAN NOVEL: THEORY AND PRACTICE IN THE NOVELS OF GEORGE ELIOT, THOMAS HARDY AND HENRY JAMES (Cambridge: Cambridge University Press, 1978) 97–126

Sound but not startling observations on H's adaptation of tragedy in the novel. H is shown to incorporate many of the forms and themes of classical tragedy (reversals, fate, unity of structure). Chapter 5 is devoted to H and discusses his four tragedies (*RN, MC, T, JO*), each receiving about half-a-dozen pages of attention. A vast topic is ably treated here, and its sensible approach can be safely recommended to the undergraduate.

587 Lodge, David
'Thomas Hardy as a Cinematic Novelist', THOMAS
HARDY AFTER FIFTY YEARS, ed. Lance St John
Butler (London: Macmillan, 1977) 78–89, expanded from
'Thomas Hardy and Cinematographic Form', *Novel* 7 (1974)
246–54. The later version is reprinted in Lodge's
WORKING WITH STRUCTURALISM: ESSAYS AND
REVIEWS ON NINETEENTH- AND TWENTIETH-
CENTURY LITERATURE (London: Routledge & Kegan
Paul, 1981) 95–105

H anticipated film in that he is a writer who 'deliberately
renounces some of the freedom of representation and report
afforded by the verbal medium, who imagines and presents
his materials in primarily visual terms, and whose visualisa-
tions correspond in some significant respect to the visual
effects characteristic of film'. He thus creates a 'visualised
world that is both recognisably "real" and yet more vivid,
intense and dramatically charged than our ordinary perception'. (Extensive analysis of opening chapters of *RN*.)

588 Page, Norman
'Hardy's Deathbeds', THOMAS HARDY ANNUAL No. 3,
ed. Norman Page (London: Macmillan, 1985) 93–110

H avoids death-scenes in his work more often than not, 'and
while making considerable fictional use of the *fact* of death
Hardy seizes very few opportunities of describing the *act* of
dying'. Yet he shows no reluctance to contemplate a corpse
or a grave, for he is more interested in the 'static, pictorial
aspect of the dead' than in the dramatic process of dying.
[Examines six major novels.]

589 Page, Norman
'Hardy and "the world of little things"', THOMAS
HARDY ANNUAL No. 5, ed. Norman Page (London:
Macmillan, 1987) 119–36

Excellent discussion of the use which H makes of 'the daily
world of solid objects', especially those ' "transparent things,
through which the past shines"' (Nabokov) or objects
associated with intense feelings.

590   Peck, John
       'Hardy's Novel Endings', *Journal of the Eighteen Nineties
       Society* no. 9 (1978) 10–15

       Discusses the endings of *MC, W, T* and *JO* to show how H
       self-consciously exploits the artificiality of his conclusions 'to
       modify our sense of the works as a whole'.

591   Pinion, F. B.
       'The Ranging Vision', THOMAS HARDY AFTER FIFTY
       YEARS, ed. Lance St John Butler (London: Macmillan,
       1977) 1–12

       Wide-ranging and succinct account of H's vision which
       extends from the minute to the universal, the local to the
       general. 'The range of Hardy's vision is multiple, and the
       result is frequent, sometimes juxtaposed, changes of perspec-
       tive.'

592   Rehder, R. M.
       'The Form of Hardy's Novels', THOMAS HARDY AFTER
       FIFTY YEARS, ed. Lance St John Butler (London:
       Macmillan, 1977) 13–27

       H 'thinks of form as a way of holding feeling'. It is never
       'merely a container' but is itself a feeling and allows more
       feeling. His plots, conception of character and notions of
       development all derive from this interrelation of form and
       feeling.

593   Schwarz, Daniel R.
       'Beginnings and Endings in Hardy's Major Fiction',
       CRITICAL APPROACHES TO THE FICTION OF
       THOMAS HARDY, ed. Dale Kramer (London:
       Macmillan, 1979) 17–35

       Ontological approach shows how H's works have the capacity
       to draw readers into their own reality. The world of the
       novels is a closed one in which the endings fulfil the prophecy
       of the beginnings, implying no prospect of any essential
       change. Lacking any traditional benevolent resolution, the
       endings 'confirm rather than transfigure what precedes and
       reject the notion that experience brings wisdom and

maturity'. All the major novels are cogently and succinctly discussed. An excellent essay.

594   Schwarz, Daniel R.
'The Narrator as Character in Hardy's Major Fiction',
Modern Fiction Studies 18 (Summer 1972) 155–72

The major novels dramatise the development of the narrative voice away from the perspective of the rural world into the 'intellectual crosswinds' of the nineteenth century. H was increasingly concerned with social and intellectual issues and his narrators become 'the chroniclers of patterns of history that Hardy viewed with despair'. In *MC*, for instance, the narrator abandons his pretensions of writing classical tragedy when he discovers the pettiness and commercialism of the world which is displacing Henchard.
[Discusses all major novels. Especially perceptive about *MC* and *JO*.]

595   Scott, James F.
'Spectacle and Symbol in Thomas Hardy's Fiction',
Philological Quarterly 44 (1965) 527–44

H's symbolism derives from his power to refine Gothic spectacle. At his worst, he merely contrives some grand gloomy tableau (cliff-hanging in *PBE*, thunderstorm in *FMC*). His most successful spectacles are organised around an architectural remain or imposing landscape, and 'a rich concentration of images symbolically extends the reach of his dramatic energy'. (Full account of the ampitheatre in *MC*, the dice game in *RN*, Stonehenge in *T* and Jude's entry into Christminster. A fluent and far from uncritical analysis of H's tendency towards 'sublime' spectacle.)

596   Spivey, Ted R.
'Thomas Hardy's Tragic Hero', *Nineteenth-Century Fiction*
9:3 (December 1954) 179–91

The tragedy of the great novels resides in their heroes' passionate defiance of fate and their final, understanding acceptance of it. For H, tragedy is above all the defeat of the romantic hero's desire to reach a higher spiritual state.
[Discusses *RN, MC, T, JO*.]

597   Sumner, Rosemary
'Some Surrealist Elements in Hardy's Prose and Verse',
THOMAS HARDY ANNUAL No. 3, ed. Norman Page
(London: Macmillan, 1985) 39–53

Interesting account of H's visual techniques (disproportion-
ing, enlargement and diminution) and their kinship with
surrealism. 'It is entirely appropriate that his claim to be an
innovator is based on his way of looking.'

598   Swigg, Richard
LAWRENCE, HARDY, AND AMERICAN
LITERATURE (London: Oxford University Press, 1972)
3–31, 58–80

Describes H's 'confusion of purpose' in his tragic novels, his
'basic misgiving' and 'hesitancy in the art' leading to 'an
imprecise metaphysic or an approximate "impression"'. H
struggles and fails to reconcile conflicts of consciousness.
Mainly on *RN, T* and *JO*. A chapter is devoted to
Lawrence's *Study of Thomas Hardy* (144).

599   Wittenberg, Judith Bryant
'Early Hardy Novels and the Fictional Eye', *Novel* 16:2
(1983) 151–64

The early fiction is notable for the characters' 'compulsion to
peep and eavesdrop', and such moments of 'eruptive visual
trauma' are related to the 'psychotics' of H's writing. These
crucial and disturbing voyeuristic scenes express many of his
'psychological and epistemological concerns'. Principally on
DR and *PBE*, some discussion of *UGT* and *FMC*.

600   Zabel, Morton Dauwen
'Hardy in Defense of His Art: The Aesthetic of
Incongruity', *Southern Review,* Thomas Hardy Centennial
Edition 6 (Summer 1940) 125–49. Rewritten with same title
in CRAFT AND CHARACTER: TEXTS, METHOD,
AND VOCATION IN MODERN FICTION (New York:
Viking Press, 1957) 70–96; reprinted in Albert J. Guerard
(ed.) (93) 24–45

Celebrated and often brilliant essay. The radical quality in
H's work derives 'from the conjunction, in his temperament,

of conformist and skeptical tendencies; in his humanism, of stoic acquiescence with moral protest; in his response to human character, of a kinship with gifted, rebellious, or destructive aberrations from the human norm as against his sympathy with the rudimentary types and stable humors of the folk'. This 'ambivalence of temper' means that discordance is central to his work: 'he inherited the aesthetic disorder of the age, its unresolved antipathies, its sprawling appetite for life'. (1957 version)

Textual studies

601   Beach, Joseph Warren
'Bowdlerized Versions of Hardy' *PMLA* 36 (December 1921) 632–43

Details many of H's revisions from serial to novel form, showing especially his caution and delicacy in depicting sexual matters.

602   Gatrell, Simon
'Hardy, House-Style, and the Aesthetics of Punctuation', THE NOVELS OF THOMAS HARDY, ed. Anne Smith (London: Vision Press, 1979) 169–92

Absorbing scholarly textual study of the changes in punctuation made to H's manuscripts at the whim of individual compositors. Concentrating on *UGT* and *T*, Gatrell persuasively demonstrates how H's punctuation is intended 'for the ear', trying to catch the cadences of his characters' speech.

603   Gibson, James
'Hardy and his Readers', THOMAS HARDY: THE WRITER AND HIS BACKGROUND, ed. Norman Page (London: Bell & Hyman, 1980) 192–218

Scholarly and entertaining account of H's constant duel with Grundyism and Victorian morality. H evolved three techniques to cope with the puritan ban on explicitness: suggestive imagery, different versions of the same novel and 'Grundy revisions' which would avoid giving offence. H made a virtue out of such necessities which obliged him to be indirect and subtle rather than naïvely outspoken.

604   Kramer, Dale
'Editing Hardy's Novels', THOMAS HARDY ANNUAL
No. 5, ed. Norman Page (London: Macmillan, 1987) 22–37

Reflections on his edition of *W*, and suggestions on how a general edition of H's works might proceed.

605   Schweik, Robert C.
'Current Problems in Textual Scholarship on the Works of Thomas Hardy', *English Literature in Transition* 14 (1971) 239–46

Denies that the Wessex edition of the novels (1912–13) is authoritative, as was long assumed. Schweik makes an entirely convincing demonstration of the need for a thorough re-editing of the texts.

606   Schweik, R. C.
'Thomas Hardy: Fifty Years of Textual Scholarship',
THOMAS HARDY AFTER FIFTY YEARS, ed. Lance St John Butler (London: Macmillan, 1977) 135–48

Invaluable survey of textual analysis, descriptive bibliography and editing. Detailed and evaluative comments on the first fifty years of textual scholarship.

607   Schweik, Robert C., and Piret, Michael
'Editing Hardy', *Browning Institute Studies* 9 (1981) 15–41

General survey of present state of the scholarly editing of H's texts. Focuses on the question of copy-text, with special reference to *FMC*.

Language and style

608   Chapman, Raymond
THE TREATMENT OF SOUNDS IN LANGUAGE AND

LITERATURE (London: André Deutsch; Oxford: Basil
Blackwell, 1984) passim.

Especially interesting on H's presentation of dialect, which
Chapman believes is superior to that of William Barnes in
that H gives only 'a few pointers to pronunciation' and
largely eschews deviant spelling.

609   Elliott, Ralph W. V.
THOMAS HARDY'S ENGLISH (Oxford: Basil Blackwell,
1984)

Fascinating study of the singularities of H's language and
vocabulary, concentrating on 'the raw materials of Hardy's
English, his words, where he found them and how he used
them'. It is both ancient and modern, stilted archaic and
contemporary colloquial, and it 'manages to be Anglo-Saxon
Wessex and Victorian Dorset rolled into one'.

610   Ingham, Patricia
'Dialect in the Novels of Hardy and George Eliot',
LITERARY ENGLISH SINCE SHAKESPEARE, ed.
George Watson (London, Oxford and New York: Oxford
University Press, 1970) 347–63

H uses dialect to express both the social inferiority of
characters and, on occasions, their capacity for deep feeling.
Interesting account of when and why H's characters use
dialect.

611   Page, Norman
'Hardy and the English Language', THOMAS HARDY:
THE WRITER AND HIS BACKGROUND, ed. Norman
Page (London: Bell & Hyman, 1980) 151–72

Fascinating study of H's 'intensive attention to style' and
sustained concern with 'questions of language, tone and
texture'. Page believes that H's occasional lapses and infelici-
ties are the result of 'trying too hard' or 'not knowing when
he has said enough'. Strong defence of H's handling of
dialect and his 'sudden and rapid transitions from one kind of
language to another'.

612   Page, Norman
        SPEECH IN THE ENGLISH NOVEL (London: Longman,
        1973) passim

        Excellent study of H's use of dialogue in the fiction.
        Especially interesting on the speech of H's rustics which 'has
        a real relationship to spontaneous speech'.

613   Salter, C. H.
        'Hardy's "Pedantry"', *Nineteenth-Century Fiction* 28:2
        (September 1973) 145–64

        Defends H's use of pedantic, Latinate or pompous language
        in the fiction. Such words are often used ironically or
        comically to deny the apparent contrast between 'trivial'
        Wessex and the 'important' world outside. 'If Wessex has the
        thing, and learning only supplies the name, then learning
        without Wessex is absurd.' The scholarly allusions insist that
        the people of Wessex are no less great or complex than the
        figures of myth or history. A copiously illustrated study, with
        catalogues of evidence.

Hardy and women

614   Childers, Mary
        'Thomas Hardy, the Man who "Liked" Women', *Criticism*
        23:4 (Fall 1981) 317–34

        On the function of women in H's fiction, especially interest-
        ing in its discussion of H's 'inadvertent, defensive misogyny'.

615   Cunningham, Gail
        'Thomas Hardy: New Women for Old', THE NEW
        WOMAN AND THE VICTORIAN NOVEL (London:
        Macmillan; New York: Harper & Row, 1978) 80–118

        H's portrayal of 'advanced womanhood' is ambiguous, and
        his ideas on sex and marriage 'seem to pull him uncomfort-
        ably in different directions'. His heroines are often fickle,
        vain and coy, but they are usually more intelligent than the
        men and enjoy a degree of independence. Sue Bridehead, in
        JO, emerges as a hybrid, 'part contemporary feminist, and

part the traditional Hardy heroine'. Valuable discussion of reviewers' reactions to the female characters. Concentrates chiefly on *W, T* (dull commentary) and *JO* (intelligent and informed analysis of Sue).

616   Humm, Maggie
'Gender and Narrative in Thomas Hardy', *Thomas Hardy Year Book* no. 11 (1984) 41–8

H's avoidance of an organised and comfortably realistic form for his novels indicates his uncertainty about how to portray his female characters. Far from endorsing the closed world of the realistic novel, H creates a deliberately awkward plot which pits male expectations and attitudes against female images, the result being 'the physical or mental destruction of woman'. Humm is largely in sympathy with H's portrayal of Tess and Sue Bridehead (to which her essay is exclusively devoted).

617   McGhee, Richard D.
' "Swinburne Planteth, Hardy Watereth": Victorian Views of Pain and Pleasure in Human Sexuality', *Tennessee Studies in Literature* 27 (1984) 83–107

Swinburne and H both learned early that they 'could not speak the truth of love, in its essential sexuality', without attracting puritan criticism. H's attitude towards the pain and pleasure of sexuality is shaped by his strong sense of the passage of time – present pain from old pleasures. McGhee devotes half of this article to H, especially *JO*: 'Sue Bridehead is certainly an interesting literary character, and her special, even perverse, sexual nature marks an advance in literary analysis of human sexuality.'

618   Miles, Rosalind
'The Women of Wessex', THE NOVELS OF THOMAS HARDY, ed. Anne Smith (London: Vision Press, 1979) 23–44

Surveys H's presentation of women. Curiously old-fashioned and rather gushing account at times – 'Hardy succeeded in tapping the vein of trembling wondering love which . . . never ceased to quiver.'

619   Poole, Adrian
       ' "Men's Words" and Hardy's Women', *Essays in Criticism*
       31 (1981) 328–45

       H's women are 'purposively blurred and blurring', vague and
       coarse, too remote and too close. 'The middle distance
       between these words turns out to be a frontier, and the
       trouble and excitement Hardy's women cause is in their
       refusal to be accommodated by these men's words as they
       cross and re-cross that middle distance between the vague
       and the coarse. The threat they pose is their ability to suggest
       that this middle-distance-frontier is a no-man's land which
       exists in *men's* minds and *men's* words.'

620   Rogers, Katharine
       'Women in Thomas Hardy', *Centennial Review* 19:4 (1975)
       249–58

       Takes H to task for his 'misogynistic stereotypes'. Principally
       on Tess ('the least flawed of Hardy's protagonists, but also
       the least human') and Sue (her inconsistency 'is presented as
       intrinsic to her feminine nature').

621   Stubbs, Patricia
       WOMEN AND FICTION: FEMINISM AND THE
       NOVEL 1880–1920 (Brighton, Sussex: Harvester Press,
       1979; pbk London: Methuen, 1981) 58–87 and passim

       H is a 'study in contradiction' for there exists 'a struggle in
       the fiction between available literary and sexual images and
       Hardy's efforts to portray real women [who] demonstrate
       convincingly women's predicament in society'. Sound but
       rarely stimulating discussion of H's portrayal of women in
       RN, W, T and *JO*.

Hardy and religion

622   Creighton, T. R. M.
       'Some Thoughts on Hardy and Religion', THOMAS
       HARDY AFTER FIFTY YEARS, ed. Lance St John
       Butler (London: Macmillan, 1977) 64–77

H was confused between logically humanist and traditionally religious values, between his 'pre-lapsarian intuition and a conscious mind committed to frustrating it'.

623   Cunningham, Valentine
      EVERYWHERE SPOKEN AGAINST: DISSENT IN THE
      VICTORIAN NOVEL (Oxford: Clarendon Press, 1975)
      passim

      Discusses H's attitude to religious dissent and the non-conformist churches (the Baptists in *L*, Alec d'Urberville's Methodism in *T*, 'The Distracted Preacher').

Hardy and Philosophy

624   Butler, Lance St John
      'How It Is for Thomas Hardy', THOMAS HARDY
      AFTER FIFTY YEARS, ed. Lance St John Butler
      (London: Macmillan, 1977) 116–25

      H, like Shakespeare, presents a picture of the world that does not conform to any predetermined cosmology, and the endings of the six major novels show him increasingly abandoning any providential structure or plan of justice. While he may *seem* to be a determined pessimist, 'the purpose of his structure is always to reveal the ultimate absence of structure'.

625   Daiches, David
      SOME LATE VICTORIAN ATTITUDES, The Ewing
      Lectures, University of California at Los Angeles, 1967
      (London: André Deutsch; New York: Norton, 1969) 68–86

      Sound comments on H's fundamental scepticism. H's chief interest was not social or economic change, but rather man's subjection to time and the disparity between his nature and his fate.

626   De Laura, David J.
      ' "The Ache of Modernism" in Hardy's Later Novels',
      Journal of English Literary History 34 (1967) 380–99

Scholarly and convincing attempt to portray H as an original and complex thinker, whose anatomy of the modern condition centres on his ambivalent response to Matthew Arnold. In *T,* for instance, Angel Clare's 'sin, like that of the later Arnold', is 'his imperfect modernism, his slavery in the ethical sphere to "custom and conventionality"'. In *T* and *JO*, those who espouse a modern and secular rational culture must pay the price of dislocation from tradition and environment.

627   Drew, Philip
THE MEANING OF FREEDOM (Aberdeen: Aberdeen University Press, 1982)

Substantial chapter on H, in the context of a wide-ranging discussion of English writers and their treatment of free will and determinism.

628   Eliot, T.S.
'Poetry and Propaganda', *Bookman* (New York) 70 (February 1930) 595–602

Very critical of H's mechanistic philosophy: 'Hardy has exploited determinism to extract his esthetic values from the contemplation of a world in which values do not count.' H ought to have had a better philosophy or no philosophy.

629   Holloway, John
THE VICTORIAN SAGE: STUDIES IN ARGUMENT (London: Macmillan; New York: St Martin's Press, 1953; reprinted Hamden, Conn.: Archon Books, 1962 and New York: Norton Paperback, 1965) 244–89

Celebrated study showing how H's novels embody 'a definite though unobtrusive sense of values'. Repeatedly, his novels show the 'determined system of things which ultimately controls human affairs without regard for human wishes'. To live naturally, H believes, is 'to live in continuity with one's whole biological and geographical environment'. The 'good' are those who enjoy this continuity with nature, the 'bad' are those who have lost it and pursue 'some private self-generated dream instead'. The most complete expressions of

H's 'impression' of life are to be found in *FMC, RN, W* and *T. JO* and *MC* are complementary in giving voice 'only to half of Hardy's whole view of life'.

630   Pinion, F. B.
'Chance, Choice, and Charity: Hardy and the Future of Civilisation', THOMAS HARDY AND THE MODERN WORLD (104) 71–89

Conventional musings on H's views of fate, coincidence, necessity and character.

631   Swann, Furse
'Thomas Hardy and the "Appetite for Joy" ', *Powys Review* 3:4 (No. 12) (Spring 1983) 39–47

Reflections on H's positive vision, stressing his love of song, the significance of the seemingly trivial and the importance of love and humanity. Unpedantic celebration of H.

632   Wright, Walter F.
'A Novel is an Impression, not an Argument', BUDMOUTH ESSAYS ON THOMAS HARDY [etc. – see 103] 154–67

On H's philosophical speculations. The work gives us 'Hardy's *impression* of the human predicament and of the strength and resiliency of the human spirit, which can endure'.

Hardy and other writers

633   Bawer, Bruce
'Two on a Tower: Hardy and Yeats', *Yeats Eliot Review* 7 (1982) 91–108

On the relationship of the two poets, and the marked similarities of tone, vision, diction, and subject-matter in their work. They did not admire each other, and Bawer seems to prefer Yeats.

634   Grundy, Joan
'Hardy and Milton', THOMAS HARDY ANNUAL No. 3,
ed. Norman Page (London: Macmillan, 1985) 3–14

Describes the influence of Milton on *T* (Tess as Eve), *JO*
(Milton's Divorce pamphlets) and *D* (which resembles
Paradise Lost in 'the sheer reach of its vision').

635   Irvine, Peter L.
'Faulkner and Hardy', *Arizona Quarterly* 26 (1970) 357–65

Faulkner is seen as H's twin in their concern with old
institutions threatened with change. Tradition for both
writers involves a pattern of cultural rise and fall.

636   Kinkead-Weekes, Mark
'Lawrence on Hardy', THOMAS HARDY AFTER FIFTY
YEARS, ed. Lance St John Butler (London: Macmillan,
1977) 90–103

Forceful defence of the relevance of Lawrence's *Study* (144)
to critics of H in that, 'though Lawrence is the traveller, it is
Hardy who defines the journey'. H is a 'profoundly creative
influence' on Lawrence, although finally 'no two novelists, in
being so like each other, are in fact so different'.

637   Laird, J. T.
'Approaches to Fiction: Hardy and Henry James',
THOMAS HARDY ANNUAL No. 2, ed. Norman Page
(London: Macmillan, 1984) 41–60

Clear and initially rather simple opposition of H and James,
contrasting their theories on realism, morality and form in
fiction. Proceeds to an interesting comparison of Tess and
Isabel Archer, stressing H's Aristotelian conception of the
former, who is accordingly shown to be typical and universal.

638   Langbaum, Robert
'Hardy and Lawrence', THOMAS HARDY ANNUAL
No. 3, ed. Norman Page (London: Macmillan, 1985) 15–38

Compares H and D. H. Lawrence, concentrating on the
latter's *Study* (144) to show what he learned in his own

writing from H. Interesting 'Lawrentian' analyses of *T* and
JO, concluding that H, born a generation later, would have
been 'a novelist very much like D. H. Lawrence'.

639   Luedtke, Luther S.
       'Sherwood Anderson, Thomas Hardy and "Tandy" ',
       Modern Fiction Studies 20 (Winter 1974–75) 531–40

Both authors created 'mythic communities' in which modern
technology and commerce fragment rural lives. Anderson's
'Tandy' (in *Winesburg, Ohio*) contains a character named
Tom Hart, who resembles Jude.

640   Nettels, Elsa
       'Howells and Hardy', *Colby Library Quarterly* 20:2 (June
       1984) 107–22

On the friendship of the two writers, their literary aims and
theories.

641   Orel, Harold
       'Hardy, Kipling and Haggard', *English Literature in
       Transition* 25 (1982) 232–48

Describes the 'beneficial' relationships which the three
writers enjoyed with each other.

642   Peck, John
       'Hardy and Joyce: A Basis for Comparison', *Ariel* 12:2
       (April 1981) 71–85

H anticipates Joyce intermittently in three areas: 'they share
an interest in how a large form, such as epic or tragedy,
relates to life. They both scrutinize the various styles which
can be employed in a narrative, with an awareness of these as
strategies for structuring the world. And they both encourage
us to consider how the individual written word relates to the
world'. Most of the illustrations of H's self-conscious mode
are drawn from *MC*. Where the two authors part company is
in H's growing feeling that art in the novel was 'a senseless
playing with patterns'. An interesting and cautious attempt to
explain the co-existence in H's novels of the realistic/visual/

direct and the self-conscious and extremely indirect modes of writing.

643   Salter, K. W.
'Lawrence, Hardy, and "The Great Tradition" ', *English*, 22 (Summer 1973) 60–5

In his essay on H (see 144), Lawrence responded to something in the novels 'which he recognized as true for and in himself'. Both men portray thought as a disease of the flesh. Lawrence was correct to identify H's defect as a refusal to 'give fair play all round'. *T* and *JO* especially suffer from H's willingness to subdue his art to a philosophy, 'the presumption of inevitability without the communication of any sense of inevitability. We are given the results without the evidence'. [An intelligent account of why Lawrence 'was impelled to write on Hardy as he did'. Notably harsh on the 'obtrusive' doctrine of *T*].

Florence Hardy's *The Life of Thomas Hardy*

644   Buckler, William E.
'Thomas Hardy's Sense of Self: The Poet Behind the Autobiographer in *The Life of Thomas Hardy*', *Prose Studies* 1:3 (May 1980) 69–86

Outstanding account of H's 'illusive gesture' in composing his *Life*, which 'begins to take on the character of a new fiction'. By *choosing* to be seen as he wished to be seen, H 'became a textual Thomas Hardy', thereby enabling him to preserve the 'well-shaped open-endedness' of his work: it would be impossible, for instance, to identify the 'I' of his lyrics with a supposedly real man, since 'the real Thomas Hardy is still the textual Thomas Hardy', a self-image which H himself constructed in his *Life*.

645   Gregor, Ian and Irwin, Michael
'Your Story or Your Life?: Reflections on Thomas Hardy's Autobiography', THOMAS HARDY ANNUAL No. 2, ed. Norman Page (London: Macmillan, 1984) 157–70

H's *Life* is not a memoir, apology or confession but has more in common with that 'series of seemings' found in his novels.

The autobiography is strictly a writer's life, not a book *about* a writer or his views on life. The answer to the question in the essay's title is that the *Life* is both story and life.

646   Morgan, Rosemarie
'Inscriptions of Self: Thomas Hardy and Autobiography',
THOMAS HARDY ANNUAL No. 5, ed. Norman Page
(London: Macmillan, 1987) 137–56

A semiological, occasionally turgid, study of H's *Life* (58), suggesting that, 'if Hardy eclipses the lexical "I", effacing self-referentiality to ground the self in a public persona, he does so, as we have seen, keenly conscious of the need to inscribe upon his text pointers to the private, passional self'.

647   Taylor, Richard H.
'Hardy's Disguised Autobiography', *Thomas Hardy Society Review,* 1:4 (1978) 104–9

Acute reflections on Florence Hardy's role in the composition of her *Life* (58) and the extent to which the secrecy of the operation was preserved.

Wessex and regionalism

648   Draper, R. P.
'Hardy and the Question of Regionalism', *Thomas Hardy Journal* 1:3 (October 1985) 28–40

Beginning with H's poem 'Domicilium' and progressing through an analysis of 'parochialism', 'provincialism' and 'regionalism', Draper argues that H's regionalism has a universal quality which is neither idealised nor sentimentalised.

649   Hyde, William J.
'Hardy's View of Realism: A Key to the Rustic Characters', *Victorian Studies* 2 (September 1958) 451–9

Assembles much historical evidence to show that H's Wessex is an accurate reflection of the real economic distress in rural

England. Nevertheless, H gives a selective and heightened portrayal of the rustics, and he is no simple realist.

650   Irwin, Michael and Gregor, Ian
'Either Side of Wessex', THOMAS HARDY AFTER
FIFTY YEARS, ed. Lance St John Butler (London:
Macmillan, 1977) 104–15

The beginning and end of H's career as a novelist are examined, showing how *DR* and *WB* mark significant points in H's 'imaginative journey' that 'neither began nor ended in Wessex'.

651   Keith, W. J.
'A Regional Approach to Hardy's Fiction', CRITICAL
APPROACHES TO THE FICTION OF THOMAS
HARDY, ed. Dale Kramer (London: Macmillan, 1979)
36–49

To the genre of the regional novel, H added two major features: he created a *series* of such novels, permitting a broad canvas to be painted, and he placed at the very heart of his novels those alien pressures and social changes which prevent the regional from becoming merely a local or provincial backwater. A perceptive analysis of the regional approach to the Wessex novels.

652   Millgate, Michael
'Unreal Estate: Reflections on Wessex and
Yoknapatawpha', THE LITERATURE OF REGION AND
NATION, ed. R. P. Draper (London: Macmillan, 1988)
61–80

H may not have devised and exploited the idea of 'Wessex' with such deliberation as Faulkner did in his creation of Yoknapatawpha, but he gave his Wessex enough imaginative realisation and peopled it with enough distinctively local inhabitants, possessing their own speech and their own 'customs of the country', for it to become in his readers' minds an autonomous artistic territory with its own entirely credible way of life. It was H who promoted regionalism to its special position in the English imagination.

653   Quinn, Maire A.
        'Wessex and the World', *Thomas Hardy Year Book* no. 5
        (1976) 70–5

        H was anxious to disguise his affinities with the ballad
        writers, lest he be dismissed as provincial. Consequently, he
        displays his erudition, craftsmanship and the cosmopolitan
        quality of his art. A further aesthetic result of this anxiety is
        that he constantly attempts to endow the local or regional
        aspects of his novels with 'universal resonance'. Quinn places
        H in relation to the 'local' William Barnes and the 'univer-
        salising' theories of Matthew Arnold.

654   Widdowson, Peter
        'Hardy, "Wessex", and the Making of a National Culture',
        THOMAS HARDY ANNUAL No. 4, ed. Norman Page
        (London: Macmillan, 1986) 45–69

        A provocative, self-consciously crusading attempt to lay bare
        the ideological assumptions underlying the view of H as the
        poet of rural England.

655   Williams, Raymond
        'Wessex and the Border', THE COUNTRY AND THE
        CITY (London: Chatto & Windus; New York: Oxford
        University Press, 1973) 197–214; reprinted in THE
        ENGLISH NOVEL: DEVELOPMENTS IN CRITICISM
        SINCE HENRY JAMES, ed. Stephen Hazell (London:
        Macmillan, 1978) 190–205

        Emphasises H's narrative stance as 'the educated observer
        and the passionate participant'. He eschews simple opposi-
        tions such as those between the country and the city or
        nature and industrialism, in favour of an awareness of change
        which is grasped both sociologically and psychologically: 'The
        profound disturbances that Hardy records cannot then be
        seen in the sentimental terms of neo-pastoral. The exposed
        and separated individuals, whom Hardy puts at the centre of
        his fiction, are only the most developed cases of a general
        exposure and separation. Yet they are never merely illustra-
        tions of this change in a way of life. Each has a dominant
        personal history, which in psychological terms bears a direct
        relation to the social character of change.'

[Substantially similar to Williams' 'Thomas Hardy', THE
ENGLISH NOVEL FROM DICKENS TO LAWRENCE
(London: Chatto & Windus; New York: Oxford University
Press, 1970) 95–118, parts of which are reprinted in R. P.
Draper (ed.), HARDY: THE TRAGIC NOVELS (90)
94–105.]

656   Wing, George
'Hardy and Regionalism', THOMAS HARDY: THE
WRITER AND HIS BACKGROUND, ed. Norman Page
(London: Bell & Hyman, 1980) 76–101

Sound, familiar study of H's use of Wessex and his concern
with change, restlessness and the invasion of outsiders,
ending with the view that 'a blight – affecting place and
people – seems gradually to spread over the region'.

Hardy's reading

657   Björk, Lennart A.
'Hardy and his "Literary Notes"', THOMAS HARDY
ANNUAL No. 1, ed. Norman Page (London: Macmillan,
1982) 115–28

Fascinating article by the recognised authority on H's
'Literary Notes' which H compiled throughout his writing life
and which he utilised for incidental detail and also to support
the thematic structures of his writing. H's consistency of
viewpoint is remarkable; for instance, he 'seems to have been
unable to come across a striking piece of criticism of the
Christian God without copying it down'. He shows a similar
liking for comments which endorse his own anti-realistic
aesthetic. The notes vividly illustrate H's intellectual background and extensive reading, but Björk's principal achievement is to show how 'individual entries provide us with
glimpses into his workshop'.

658   Björk, Lennart A.
'Hardy's Reading', THOMAS HARDY: THE WRITER
AND HIS BACKGROUND, ed. Norman Page (London:
Bell & Hyman, 1980) 102–27

Authoritative account of H's reading and its influence on his fiction. Björk ignores H's religious and metaphysical beliefs and concentrates instead on his reading in psychological and social matters, discussing such authors as Auguste Comte, Charles Fourier and Matthew Arnold. They influenced his 'idealistic and visionary social criticism'.

Hardy and the other arts

659   Carpenter, Richard C.
'Thomas Hardy and the Old Masters', *Boston University Studies in English* 4 (Spring 1961) 18–28

Fascinating and stimulating argument that 'the use of "painterly" methods is a primary ingredient in the creation of some of Hardy's finest scenes and most memorable effects'. H deals little in colour, but is very particular about composition, point of view, framing, perspective, spatial perception and lighting.

660   Fernando, Lloyd
'Thomas Hardy's Rhetoric of Painting', *Review of English Literature* 6 (October 1965) 62–73

'No other novel of Hardy's contains as much of the *ore* of his rhetoric of painting' as *RN*, with 'its devotion to style for its own sake' and 'largely immobile' heroine. Critical account of H's 'frequent recourse to the visual arts' in *RN*.

661   Jackson, Arlene M.
'Photography as Style and Metaphor in the Art of Thomas Hardy', THOMAS HARDY ANNUAL No. 2, ed. Norman Page (London: Macmillan, 1984) 91–109

Excellent analysis of H's references to photography. Much discussion of H's fascination with point of view, framing and selection. Ends by assessing the photographic imagery in *JO*.

662   Maidment, B. E.
'Hardy's Fiction and English Traditional Music', THOMAS HARDY ANNUAL No. 4, ed. Norman Page (London: Macmillan, 1986) 3–18

Describes H's fictional accounts of traditional music and its demise as metaphors for 'an organic community threatened by change', while acknowledging H's warnings of the dangers of extreme responsiveness to music. Especially detailed study of 'The Fiddler of the Reels'.

663   Smart, Alastair
'Pictorial Imagery in the Novels of Thomas Hardy', *Review of English Studies* ns. 12 (1961) 262–80

Important analysis of H's knowledge of the visual arts (especially Turner and Rembrandt) and his allusions to painters in the fiction. Very detailed and stimulating essay.

Nature and landscape

664   Blythe, Ronald
CHARACTERS AND THEIR LANDSCAPES (San Diego: Harcourt, 1983)

Chapters on *FMC* and *PBE*.

665   Eagleton, Terry
'Thomas Hardy: Nature as Language', *Critical Quarterly* 13:2 (Summer 1971) 155–62

Nature and the material world are a kind of language which can bear meaning and mediate between the spirit and the flesh, inner and outer, subjective and objective modes of perception. Examines the role of the heath and the fires in *RN*, and is especially astute in analysis of Tess, whose 'tragic crisis centres on a wrenching apart of personal identity and the physical body'.

666   Fletcher, Pauline
'Hardy: The Chastened Sublime', GARDENS AND GRIM RAVINES: THE LANGUAGE OF LANDSCAPE IN VICTORIAN POETRY (Princeton, N.J.: Princeton University Press, 1983) 224–46

Pedestrian account of H's poetic presentation of landscape. For H, man is a part of nature, and subject to its harsh laws.

He gives an incidental treatment of landscape as a part of human suffering, rejecting 'the aesthetic quality of scenery in favor of man's subjective vision of nature'.

667 Paterson, John
'The Continuing Miracle: Nature and Character in Thomas Hardy', BUDMOUTH ESSAYS ON THOMAS HARDY [etc. – see 103] 140–53

H singled out 'what was surprising and unusual for the data of his natural scenes and settings'. He is at his best when 'he can make the ordinary in nature extraordinary in ways that do not draw attention to themselves', heightening and intensifying reality without extravagantly rearranging it. H thus rehabilitated man and nature as a source of mystery and miracle.

668 Paterson, John
'Lawrence's Vital Source: Nature and Character in Thomas Hardy', NATURE AND THE VICTORIAN IMAGINATION, ed. U. C. Knoepflmacher and G. B. Tennyson (Berkeley: University of California Press, 1977) 455–69

Detailed but rather conventional account of H's portrayal of nature, illustrating how he 'restored the possibility of the wonder and miracle of things' (hence his special importance for Lawrence).

Hardy and social change

669 Huss, Roy
'Social Change and Moral Decay in the Novels of Thomas Hardy', *Dalhousie Review* 47 (1967) 28–44

H is deeply sceptical about the possibility of social amelioration, since society is simply 'the final expression of the Immanent Will' and therefore is subject to this 'delinquent first cause'. Wide-ranging survey of H's social criticism in the fiction, focusing especially on marriage, education and urban values.

670   Lucas, John
       'Hardy's Women', THE LITERATURE OF CHANGE:
       STUDIES IN THE NINETEENTH-CENTURY
       PROVINCIAL NOVEL (Brighton, Sussex: Harvester Press;
       New York: Barnes & Noble, 1977) 119–91

       Relates social change to individual's loss of identity. H's
       heroines tend to be viewed from the perspective of their
       lovers, usually to their detriment.

671   Pollard, Arthur
       'Hardy and Rural England', THOMAS HARDY ANNUAL
       No. 1, ed. Norman Page (London: Macmillan, 1982) 33–43

       Principally, an attack on the socio-economic approach to H
       by such critics as Douglas Brown and Raymond Williams,
       which Pollard sees as engulfing the individual in the circum-
       stances of his or her life: 'Wessex is only partly, and not most
       importantly, the scene of agricultural change in Hardy's own
       time; it is far more imperative to see it as the vast and ageless
       setting in which the tragedy of man is acted out.' Discusses
       chiefly *MC* and *T*.

672   Rosenberg, Devra Braun
       'The Shifting Balance of Community, History, and Nature
       in Thomas Hardy's Wessex Novels (1874–1896)', *Durham
       University Journal* 39 (January 1977) 59–67

       Gabriel Oak and Jude have contrasting relationships to their
       communities, yet there is a nobility and significance in both
       their lives. H judges them by different standards, for nature,
       historical continuity and community life have become
       increasingly dissonant by the time H wrote *JO*.

673   Sherman, G. W.
       'Thomas Hardy and the Agricultural Laborer',
       Nineteenth-Century Fiction 7:2 (September 1952) 111–18

       H's essay, 'The Dorsetshire Labourer', illuminates his
       portrayal of rural change, especially depopulation, in the
       novels.

674   Williams, Merryn and Raymond
'Hardy and Social Class', THOMAS HARDY: THE
WRITER AND HIS BACKGROUND, ed. Norman Page
(London: Bell & Hyman, 1980) 29–40

Sociological discussion of H's portrayal of class relations in
the major novels. H 'especially regretted the disappearance
of the relatively independent and intermediate class' into
which he himself had been born, and his work charts the
implications of mobility (especially through education) for
that class of people who had been 'bearers of a culture'.
Problems of class are also seen in H's 'deeply original and
still exceptional emphasis on work', in which 'being is
expressed in labour'.

675   Williams, Raymond
'Thomas Hardy', *Critical Quarterly* 6 (1964) 341–51

Sociological and historical approach which seeks to demolish
the view of H as a peasant and Wessex as pastoral. Rather,
the principal characters are exposed and alienated individuals
suffering the immediate effects of mobility. H is not
especially concerned with the impact of the urban on the
'timeless' rural world. A more common pattern is the relation
between the changing nature of country living, determined
partly by internal pressures, and characters separated from
the country but still inescapably connected to it, usually by
family ties. An important study.

Pastoral

676   Hunter, Shelagh
'Thomas Hardy: Character and Environment',
VICTORIAN IDYLLIC FICTION: PASTORAL
STRATEGIES (London: Macmillan, 1984) 167–208

Examines H's pastoral novels (*UGT, W, FMC*), showing H
to be 'the most inventive of modern writers of pastoral'.
Especially interesting discussion of impressionist style in *W*,
part of which is reprinted in R. P. Draper (ed.), THOMAS
HARDY: THREE PASTORAL NOVELS (91) 194–202.

677   May, Charles E.
'*Far from the Madding Crowd* and *The Woodlanders*:
Hardy's Grotesque Pastorals', *English Literature in
Transition* 17:3 (1974) 147–58

H's philosophical vision is not compatible with traditional
pastoral and is therefore distorted in these two novels, which
are 'grotesque pastorals'. Their actual endings are not the
true ones.

678   Squires, Michael
THE PASTORAL NOVEL: STUDIES IN GEORGE
ELIOT, THOMAS HARDY, AND D. H. LAWRENCE
(Charlottesville: University of Virginia Press, 1974) 106–29,
150–73 and passim. Extracts from Chapter 7 on *W* are
reprinted in R. P. Draper (ed.), THOMAS HARDY:
THREE PASTORAL NOVELS (91) 180–94

The two early pastoral novels, *UGT* and *FMC,* are charming
and idyllic, expressing 'full confidence in the strength of the
pastoral world to sustain itself'. They are, however, modified
pastoral in depicting realistic details of rural life and work.
W, unlike its predecessors, is 'gloomy and ironic', expressing
doubt and anxious melancholy. It contains both the idyllic
eclogue of pastoral poetry (the leisure and loves of
shepherds) and the *georgic* (the real world of farming and
productive country pursuits). Unusually detailed analysis.

Miscellaneous

679   Bailey, J. O.
'Hardy's "Mephistophelian Visitants"'', *PMLA* 61
(December 1946), 1146–84

A typological study of H's satanic intruders (Diggory Venn,
or Dare in *L*) who psychically disrupt the communities which
they invade. Sergeant Troy *(FMC)* and Farfrae *(MC)* are
interlopers whose arrival has a similar effect.

680   Bailey, J. O.
'Hardy and the Modern World', THOMAS HARDY AND
THE MODERN WORLD (104) 1–13

On the reasons for H's increasing relevance and popularity in the 1970s, especially his concern with religious, intellectual and social changes.

681   Bartle, G. F.
'Some Fresh Information about Tryphena Sparks – Thomas Hardy's Cousin', *Notes & Queries* ns. 30:4 (1983) 320–2

Prints some recently discovered letters from Tryphena in 1871 concerning her teaching career. Also prints good testimonials to her teaching ability, which make it 'unthinkable' that she could recently have had an illegitimate child by H.

682   Beckman, Richard
'A Character Typology for Hardy's Novels', *Journal of English Literary History* 30 (March 1963) 70–87

H is said to depict four main kinds of response to the world and its ironies: a character may, 'while ignoring the ironies of the world, take advantage of its occasional opportunities. Or, he may willfully resist its ironical tendencies. Or he may, under the guise of worldliness, attempt to avoid its insistent ironies. Finally he may accept the ironical and accommodate himself to its incongruities'. This is an inevitably schematic but often stimulating discussion; chiefly on *MC* but looks at all major novels. Best on Tess and Jude, who are shown each to possess all four ways of responding at different times in their lives.

683   Benson, Michael
'Moving Bodies in Hardy and Beckett', *Essays in Criticism* 34 (1984) 229–43

Rather curiously compares H's alleged lack of interest in portraying bodily movement with Samuel Beckett's dramatic techniques.

684   Bragg, Melvyn and Gittings, Robert
THOMAS HARDY (II) (East Ardsley, Yorkshire: Sussex Tapes, Educational Productions Ltd, 1975)

An excellent recorded discussion of *JO* (side 1) and the poems (side 2), done with freshness and judicious enthusiasm, and concentrating particularly on the connections between H's life and work.

685   Caless, Bryn
'Hardy's Humour', THOMAS HARDY ANNUAL No. 3, ed. Norman Page (London: Macmillan, 1985) 111–28

H's humour is 'an integral part of his artist's perception' since it often expresses incongruity and the difference between what might be and what is. Wide-ranging illustrations given.

686   Casagrande, Peter J.
' "Old Tom and New Tom": Hardy and his Biographers', THOMAS HARDY ANNUAL No. 1, ed. Norman Page (London: Macmillan, 1982) 1–32

A scholarly and occasionally contentious survey of how H has fared at the hands of his biographers. Begins with a generally dismissive review of Gittings (54), which is said to be reductive and incomplete in its relentless emphasis on 'Hardy at his worst'. Casagrande then discusses H's marginal annotations in the biographies by Hedgcock (135), Brennecke (50) and Chew (123), and proceeds to survey later biographies by focusing on their treatment of H in the years 1876–78, which produced *RN*, with its tragic handling of autobiographical materials. A very readable and exceedingly clear account of the subject.

687   Chesterton, Gilbert Keith
'Great Victorian Novelists', THE VICTORIAN AGE IN LITERATURE (London: William & Norgate; New York: Holt, 1913) 138–9, 143–5

Notorious for its depiction of H as 'the village atheist brooding and blaspheming over the village idiot'. H nevertheless needed to personify a God in order to 'give Him a piece of his mind'.

688   Clark, S. L., and Wasserman, J. N.
THOMAS HARDY AND THE TRISTRAN LEGEND,

Anglistiche Forschungen 168 (Heidelberg: Carl Winter Universitätsverlag, 1983)

Monograph on H's use of the Tristran legend in *PBE, Queen of Cornwall* and, most interestingly, *T.*

689   Collins, Philip
'Hardy and Education', THOMAS HARDY: THE WRITER AND HIS BACKGROUND, ed. Norman Page (London: Bell & Hyman, 1980) 41–75

Very thorough and clear account of H's attitude to education. His novels show how education was 'changing outlook and life-style, as well as affecting class mobility, professional procedures, and much else, at every level of society'. Interesting biographical discussion of H's own experiences, coupled with information about educational changes during his lifetime. Extensive analyses of *RN* and *JO*.

690   Coxon, Peter W.
'Hardy's Use of the Hair Motif', THOMAS HARDY ANNUAL No. 1, ed. Norman Page (London: Macmillan, 1982) 95–114

Exhaustive account of H's heroines and their hair (colour, style, symbolism, etc.).

691   Doheny, John R.
'The Youth of Thomas Hardy', THOMAS HARDY YEAR BOOK No. 12 (1984) 6–116

Long essay which seeks to challenge those who deny that there was a sexual relationship between H and Tryphena Sparks. Much impressive research on Tryphena's career at college.

692   Draper, Ronald Philip
'Hardy and Respectability', AN ENGLISH MISCELLANY, PRESENTED TO W. S. MACKIE, ed. Brian S. Lee (Cape Town, London, New York: Oxford University Press, 1977) 179–207

Draper examines the contradictory strains in H's work which both attack the hypocritical pretensions associated with respectability and sympathetically identify with characters for whom it is a psychological necessity. He explores this theme with reference to the poetry and the fiction, including *UGT*, 'The Romantic Adventures of a Milkmaid', *HE* and *MC*.

693   Eliot, T. S.
AFTER STRANGE GODS: A PRIMER OF MODERN HERESY (London: Faber & Faber; New York: Harcourt Brace, 1934) 59–62; reprinted in POINTS OF VIEW (London: Faber & Faber, 1941)

Famous, unctuous dismissal of H: 'He seems to me to have written as nearly for the sake of "self-expression" as a man well can; and the self which he had to express does not strike me as a particularly wholesome or edifying matter of communication.' H's style 'touches sublimity without ever having passed through the stage of being good'.

694   Enstice, Andrew
'The Fruit of the Tree of Knowledge', THE NOVELS OF THOMAS HARDY, ed. Anne Smith (London: Vision Press, 1979) 9–22

On H's Job-like quest for 'a meaning in human existence', showing how 'the images of the Old Testament serve Hardy well'. Brief analyses of all the major novels.

695   Escuret, Annie
'Hardy's Reputation in France', THOMAS HARDY ANNUAL No. 2, ed. Norman Page (London: Macmillan, 1984) 191–5

Laments critical neglect of H in France. Useful bibliography of criticism and translations of H in French, 1954–82.

696   Foote, I. P.
'Thomas Hardy in Russian Translation and Criticism (to 1978)', *Thomas Hardy Year Book* no. 11 (1984) 6–27

H has been available in Russian translation since the 1890s, and he seems often regarded as a critic of a bourgeois society.

697   Gilmour, Robin
THE NOVEL IN THE VICTORIAN AGE: A MODERN
INTRODUCTION (London: Edward Arnold, 1986) 185–95

Chapter 7, 'The Ache of Modernism', contains a succinct and well-written account of the major novels, highlighting H's debt to Darwinism, his conversion of the 'sensation' novel to a vehicle of poetic impressionism and his engagement with contemporary issues. The brief treatment of *T* is excellent.

698   Gregor, Ian and Lodge, David
THE NOVELS OF THOMAS HARDY (East Ardsley,
Yorkshire: Sussex Tapes, Educational Productions Ltd,
1971)

A leisurely, but illuminating, recorded discussion, nicely balanced between the general characteristics of H's fiction (side 1) and more detailed commentary of three novels, *FMC, RN* and *T* (side 2).

699   Gregor, Ian and Lodge, David
'Thomas Hardy', QUESTIONS IN LITERATURE: THE
ENGLISH NOVEL, ed. Cedric Watts (London: Sussex
Books, 1976) 95–110

Lively critical dialogue, centring on H's cinematic qualities, his regionalism and the role of the rustic characters.

700   Halliday, F.E.
'Thomas Hardy: The Man in his Work', THOMAS
HARDY AFTER FIFTY YEARS, ed. Lance St John
Butler (London: Macmillan, 1977) 126–34

Conventional musings on H's revelation of himself in his writings.

701   Holloway, John
'Hardy's Major Fiction', FROM JANE AUSTEN

TO JOSEPH CONRAD: ESSAYS COLLECTED IN
MEMORY OF JAMES T. HILLHOUSE, ed. Robert C.
Rathburn and Martin Steinmann, Jr (Minneapolis:
University of Minnesota Press, 1958) 234–45; Reprinted in
Holloway's THE CHARTED MIRROR: LITERARY
AND CRITICAL ESSAYS (London: Routledge & Kegan
Paul, 1960), 94–107; and in HARDY: A COLLECTION
OF CRITICAL ESSAYS, ed. Albert J. Guerard (93), 52–62

Distinguished essay traces H's pessimism, the development
towards the 'realization that that earlier way [of rural life] did
not possess the inner resources upon which to fight for its
existence. The old order was not just a less powerful mode of
life than the new, but ultimately helpless before it through
inner defect'. Looks especially at *MC* (Henchard as tamed
beast) and *T* (Tess as hunted animal driven, in Darwinian
terms, to extinction).

702   Horne, Lewis B.
' "The Art of Renunciation" in Hardy's Novels', *Studies in
the Novel* 4:4 (Winter 1972) 556–67

H's earlier novels show renunciation as a positive act worthy
of reward, but the later works show it to be ineffectual. A
new and destructive kind of renunciation is seen in *JO*.

703   Jones, Lawrence O.
'Hardy's Unwritten Second Sensation Novel', THOMAS
HARDY ANNUAL No. 2, ed. Norman Page (London:
Macmillan, 1984) 30–40

H apparently planned to follow his first novel, *DR*, with
another sensation novel, whose surviving outline shows that
it was to feature bigamy, rich widows, disguise and a happy
marriage at the end. Poor sales and reviews of *DR* probably
made H concentrate on *UGT* instead.

704   Kettle, Arnold
HARDY THE NOVELIST: A RECONSIDERATION,
The W. D. Thomas Memorial Lecture (Singleton Park,
Swansea: University College of Swansea, 1966)

H, like Dickens, is a great writer who does not easily fit into
academic categories. He embodies the contradiction between

the conservative and the radical. The so-called 'provincial gaucheness' is an intrinsic part of his effect. The urban is set against the rural, but the latter is not idealised. Nature is 'almost always used as a contrast with ideas'.

705   Kramer, Dale
        'Making Approaches to Hardy', CRITICAL
        APPROACHES TO THE FICTION OF THOMAS
        HARDY, ed. Dale Kramer (London: Macmillan, 1979)
        1–16

Valuable introduction to the critical strategies adopted by writers in this collection of essays, evaluating the structuralist, deconstructionist, psychological, formalist and feminist approaches to H. Kramer believes that H's concern with the 'multiple connotations of details and the virtually limitless interconnections within a novel' invites those modern approaches which record the evasiveness of the single meaning.

706   Larkin, Philip
        'Wanted: Good Hardy Critic', *Critical Quarterly* 8 (1966)
        174–9

A damning and hugely readable review of books on H by Morrell (149) and Weber (70). Larkin asks why H does not attract the best modern critics or at least ones who can write; perhaps it is because H is simple, while modern criticism thrives on the difficult. The real critic of H must primarily address 'the centrality of suffering', which H regarded as ' "true" ' and as the mark of the superior spiritual character. Larkin ends with a rousing defence of the poetry: ''May I trumpet the assurance that one reader at least would not wish Hardy's *Collected Poems* a single page shorter, and regards it as many times over the best body of poetic work this century so far has to show.'

707   Lindgren Charlotte,
        'Thomas Hardy: Grim Facts and Local Lore', *Thomas Hardy Journal* 1:3 (October 1985) 18–27

On H's fascination with morbid local tales, hangings and transportation. Old local newspapers provide much historical fact, against which one can measure H's reliance on memory and oral history.

708   Miller, J. Hillis
FICTION AND REPETITION: SEVEN ENGLISH NOVELS (Oxford: Basil Blackwell, 1982) 116–46, 147–75

Contains revised versions of Miller's articles on *T* (309) and *WB* (1).

709   Morrell, Roy
'Mr. Philip Larkin, Tess and Thomas Hardy', *Thomas Hardy Journal* 1:1 (January 1985) 40–6

Spirited, if tardy, reply to Larkin's 1966 review of his book (706). Morrell repeats that he sees Tess 'as a victim not of blind fate, but of human agency, of Victorian preconceptions, shared by Angel, concerning women and marriage; a victim too of her own fatalism (not of Fate)'.

710   Mudford, Peter
THE ART OF CELEBRATION (London: Faber & Faber, 1979) 47–60

Persistent attempt to find an optimistic and positive H; e.g. on Tess – 'Hardy does not permit his vision of joy and reconciliation to end with his heroine's execution.'

711   Osborne, L. MacKenzie
'The "Chronological Frontier" in Thomas Hardy's Novels', *Studies in the Novel* 4:4 (Winter 1972) 543–55

H interprets the clash between ancient and modern by contrasting two concepts of time–preserver and destroyer. The separation of these two times is often precarious, and the later novels regard the Victorian present as destructive, eradicating the ancient past of Wessex.

712   Pinion, F. B.
'Hardy and Myth', BUDMOUTH ESSAYS ON THOMAS HARDY [etc. – see 103] 125–39

Examines functioning of images from four mythologies in four novels: Greek mythology in *RN*, Norse in *W*, Christian in *JO* and H's own mythology (rooted in Comte's Positivism) in *T*.

713   Reed, John
VICTORIAN CONVENTIONS (Athens, Ohio: Ohio University Press, 1975) passim

H breaks with convention in his treatment of women, struggling scholars, marriage, coincidences, death, orphans, the past, the occult, etc.

714   Siemens, Lloyd
'Hardy Among the Critics: the Annotated Scrap Books', THOMAS HARDY ANNUAL No. 2, ed. Norman Page (London: Macmillan, 1984) 187–90

Interesting account of H's annotations to reviews of his work reveals his anti-feminist bias in his response to criticism and his sensitivity about reviews of his poetry (but not his novels). H seems very thin-skinned.

715   Southerington, F. R.
'Lives, Letters, and the Failure of Criticism, 1928–72', *Agenda* 10:2–3 (Spring–Summer 1972) 11–18

Interesting snapshot of the state of current H criticism. Pugnacious at times, and sympathetic to Lois Deacon (52).

716   Stewart, J. I. M.
'Hardy', EIGHT MODERN WRITERS, Vol. XII of THE OXFORD HISTORY OF ENGLISH LITERATURE, ed. F. P. Wilson and Bonamy Dobree (Oxford: Clarendon Press, 1963) 19–70

Thorough and astute survey of most aspects of H's writing career – novels, poems and *D*. Only the short stories are omitted.

717   Thomas, Denis W.
'Drunkenness in Thomas Hardy's Novels', *College Language Association Journal* 28 (1984) 109–90

Unlike Dickens' tipplers, H's rustics drink because of the brutality of their environment. Drinking ceases to be a communal celebration.

718   Tristram, Philippa
'Stories in Stones', THE NOVELS OF THOMAS HARDY, ed. Anne Smith (London: Vision Press, 1979) 145–68

Thorough discussion of H's interest in architecture, his fictional portrayal of architects and his presentation of homes and their interiors.

719   Weatherby, H. L.
'Two Hardys', *Sewanee Review* 92 (1984) 162–71

Insists on the need to distinguish between the traditional and 'the agnostic, alienated modern Hardy'. The latter appears, from the documentary evidence, to be 'a petty, disagreeable, even trivial figure' who acted disgracefully towards his wives.

720   Weber, Carl J.
'Chronology in Hardy's Novels', *PMLA* 53 (March 1938) 314–20

Ten of H's novels have their own complete and independent temporal sequences (some overlap in *JO* and *WB*) which depict the passing of the nineteenth century. An interesting assertion of H's historical realism, yet see Emery (209) and Murphree and Strauch (224).

721   Weber, Carl J.
HARDY IN AMERICA: A STUDY OF THOMAS HARDY AND HIS AMERICAN READERS (Waterville, Maine: Colby College Press, 1946)

A scholarly account of American reaction to H's work as it appeared. In some ways, H has been regarded more highly there than in Britain.

722   Widdowson, Peter
        'Hardy in History: A Case Study in the Sociology of
        Literature', *Literature and History* 9:1 (Spring 1983) 3–16

Following a turgid opening, Widdowson engages with his
chief topic, 'Hardy' as a cultural and historically determined
phenomenon in the 1980s. Looks at the influence of criticism
and examination boards on H's reputation, especially on that
division of his work into major and minor novels. Suggests
that 'Hardy' has been made to fit uneasily into 'the critical
discourse of liberal-humanist realism'.

723   Woolf, Virginia
        GRANITE AND RAINBOW: ESSAYS (London: Hogarth
        Press, 1958) 25, 26–7, 94, 98, 136–7

H is a poetical, and therefore imperfect, novelist, while he
has too limited a sympathy to be a successful poet.

724   Woolf, Virginia
        'The Novels of Thomas Hardy', THE SECOND COMMON
        READER (London: Hogarth Press, 1932)

There are passages of astonishing beauty and force in every
novel H wrote. Women in his work suffer through depend-
ence on others, while men suffer through conflict with fate.
Only *JO* could be described as pessimistic. (Reprint of an
obituary appreciation.)

Index of Authors

The index numbers refer to the number of the item.

Subject and Name Index

The index numbers refer to the number of the item.

Title Index

The index numbers refer to the number of the item.